Agroterrorism: Scientific Analysis of Biological Threats to Agriculture and Food Security

Dibyendu Nayak

SPI PUBLICATIONS

Published by SPI Publications, www.spipublications.in
SPI, the SPI logo, and Split Poetry India are trademarks of SPI Publications, or its affiliates.
ISBN-13: 9978-81-990408-9-2

First Edition 2025

SPI Publications

Corporate & Editorial Office

117/2, Sector 37, Khandsa Road,
Gurgaon, Haryana 122 001
Phone: +91 98355 52940
Email: contact@spipublications.in
Website: www.spipublications.in

Processed and Printed in India

Agroterrorism: Scientific Analysis of Biological Threats to Agriculture and Food Security

Table of Conents

Chapter 1: Conceptual Framework of Agroterrorism

Dibyendu Nayak*

*School of Agriculture, Lovely Professional University, Phagwara (Punjab), India-144411

*Corresponding author: dibyendunayak05@gmail.com

Terrorist activities have become frequent in the present world, especially in the developing countries like India. It is very unfortunate that various terrorist groups kill common people and destroy public property posing a potential threat to the unity and integrity of nations as well as disturbing the roadway of development.

1.1 Definition and Classification

Agroterrorism is defined as **the deliberate introduction of harmful biological, chemical, or other agents into the agricultural ecosystem to cause damage to crops, livestock, food systems, or agricultural infrastructure, with the intention of creating fear, economic loss, and food insecurity** (Monke, 2005).

Since the primary focus moves from human populations to agricultural systems, it is commonly regarded as a subcategory of bioterrorism. However, agroterrorism is a multifaceted threat that can include physical destruction of agri-infrastructure, cyber interference with precision agriculture, and chemical sabotage.

Considering that the agriculture industry sustains not just the supply of food but also jobs, commerce, and rural social structure, the U.S. Department of Homeland Security categorizes agroterrorism as a direct attack on national economic stability (USDA, 2018).

- Generally speaking, agroterrorism can be classified as follows:

  Biological agroterrorism is the use of animal or plant diseases to interfere with agricultural production.
  Toxic substances being introduced to crops, animals, or water supplies is known as **chemical agroterrorism.**
  Digital manipulation of food supply networks, irrigation controls, or smart farming systems is known as **cyber-agroterrorism**.
  Physical agro sabotage includes the burning, poisoning, or physical destruction of agricultural machinery, storage facilities, or food delivery networks.

1.2 Scope under Bioterrorism and Ecological Warfare

Food shortages, agro-industrial collapse, and economic paralysis are the main targets of agroterrorism, whereas bioterrorism frequently focuses on harming people. According to the United Nations Biological Weapons Convention (BWC), it is illegal to use biological agents against plants or animals for hostile purposes (UNODA, 2017).

Agroterrorism, which targets entire ecosystems to ruin a region's agricultural potential, has recently been acknowledged as a type of ecological warfare. This covers intentional invasive species introduction, genetic sabotage, and water resource contamination that is essential to agriculture (Wheelis, 2002).

Additionally, agroterrorism is a low-cost, high-risk weapon in asymmetric warfare and insurgency situations because of its silent beginning and protracted incubation periods (particularly in biological cases), which make it easy to carry out and challenging to detect (Chalk, 2004).

1.3 Framework by FAO, WHO, USDA, and UNODC

The World Health Organization (WHO) and the Food and Agriculture Organization (FAO) have highlighted the importance of agro-biosecurity frameworks worldwide, particularly in developing nations with inadequate surveillance systems (FAO & WHO, 2010). These organizations recommend the establishment of:

- **Early Warning Systems (EWS)** for pest and disease outbreaks
- **Rapid Response Teams (RRTs)** for agricultural emergencies
- **International Plant Protection Agreements (IPPC protocols)** for preventing cross-border agri-biothreats

To monitor, investigate, and develop countermeasures against agroterrorism, the USDA runs the Animal and Plant Health Inspection Service (APHIS) and the National Bio and Agro-Defense Facility (NBIS) in the United States (USDA, 2018).
According to the United Nations Office on Drugs and Crime (UNODC, 2020), agroterrorism is one of the new transnational threats, particularly when terrorist organizations target agriculture in an effort to destabilize governments, interfere with food supply chains, or harm export economies.

1.4 Agroterrorism as an Emerging Domain of Non-Conventional Warfare

The idea of agroterrorism is no longer regarded as fringe. Contemporary farming systems now face new vulnerabilities as a result of precision agriculture, globalized trade, and the emergence of climate-sensitive pests. These frequently highly automated systems are vulnerable to digital sabotage, such as the hacking of irrigation grids or the generation of false weather input data for farms powered by artificial intelligence (Kesan & Hayes, 2012).

Agroterrorism is a destabilizing weapon used in contemporary non-traditional warfare. This is especially important in nations like India, where more than 50% of the population depends on agriculture for their livelihood and it accounts for about 18% of GDP (MoAFW, 2023). Economic collapse, food riots, or social unrest in rural areas could result from disruptions in this sector.

Nations such as Israel, the United States, and Australia have established strong agricultural biosecurity frameworks in recognition of agroterrorism as a serious national security threat. However, developing nations—particularly those in South Asia and sub-Saharan Africa—continue to be ill-equipped and unprepared to identify, address, or recover from such threats.

1.5 Difference Between Bioterrorism and Agroterrorism

Table 1: Bioterrorism Vs Agroterrorism

Aspect	***Bioterrorism***	***Agroterrorism***
Definition	The intentional release of biological agents to cause illness or death in humans.	The deliberate use of biological, chemical, or other agents to harm crops, livestock, or the agricultural system.
Primary Targets	Humans (individuals or populations).	Agriculture sector,crops, livestock, food systems, or ecosystems.
Agents Used	Pathogens (e.g., anthrax, smallpox, botulinum toxin).	Plant/animal diseases (e.g., Foot and Mouth Disease, Wheat Rust), pests, invasive species, toxins.
Objective	Cause panic, mass casualties, fear, or societal disruption.	Disrupt food supply chains, cause economic collapse, incite food insecurity.
Impact	Immediate loss of life, healthcare burden, social chaos.	Long-term economic damage, food shortages, rural distress, trade bans.
Detection	Often noticed quickly due to human symptoms.	Often delayed; symptoms in crops or animals take time to appear.
Typical Perpetrators	Terrorist groups, rogue states, lone actors.	Same actors, sometimes insurgent or economic warfare units.
Example Incident	2001 anthrax attacks in the U.S.	1989 California medfly attack

Conclusion of Chapter

This chapter establishes agroterrorism as a scientifically and geopolitically important topic. It draws connections between agricultural disruption and broader national and global security risks. In the following chapters, we will explore documented cases, tactics of attack, and the current state of India's preparedness.

Chapter 2: Documented Incidents and Historical Precedents

Dibyendu Nayak[1*] and Furquan Khalid[2]

[1*] School of Agriculture, Lovely Professional University, Phagwara, Punjab-144001, India

[2]School of Agriculture, Lovely Professional University, Phagwara, Punjab-144001, India

***Corresponding author: dibyendunayak05@gmail.com**

Analyzing historical events with evidence is necessary for understanding agroterrorism. This chapter provides actual instances of biosecurity lapses and agroterror incidents, broken down by target type: ecosystems, livestock, and crops. These historical examples provide important information about the evolution of agri-bioterror threats, response strategies, and vulnerabilities.

2.1 Global Incidents of Agroterrorism

2.1.1 The 1984 Oregon Salmonella Bioterrorism Case (USA)

In The Dalles, Oregon, the Rajneeshee cult purposefully contaminated salad bars with *Salmonella typhimurium* in an effort to influence a local election, making it one of the most well-known instances of agroterrorism (Torok et al., 1997). More than 750 people were affected what was initially believed to be a natural outbreak but later turned out to be a planned biological attack. Despite having a direct human impact, this event was classified as a borderline agroterror event because it was transmitted through the food supply chain and revealed significant violations of restaurant hygiene and food handling regulations.

2.1.2 2001 Foot-and-Mouth Disease Outbreak (UK)

The 2001 Foot-and-Mouth Disease (FMD) outbreak in the UK is frequently mentioned in agroterrorism studies, despite not being officially recognized as an act of terrorism, because it replicated the scope and destruction that such an attack could bring about. An estimated £8 billion was lost economically as a result of the outbreak, which resulted in the culling of over 6 million animals (Thompson et al., 2002).

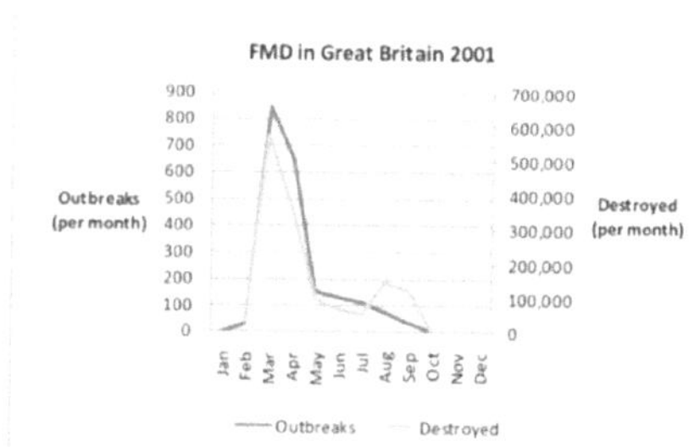

2.1.3 Operation "Vegetable Offensive" (Rhodesia, 1978-80)

It was claimed that biological warfare agents were used to contaminate rivers and crops in areas controlled by insurgents during the Rhodesian Bush War. According to post-war investigations, anthrax and *Vibrio cholerae* were used to target livestock and rural water supplies, even though this was officially unreported by international organizations (Wheelis, 2002).

2.2 FAO and WHO Investigative Records

The FAO (Food and Agriculture Organization) and WHO (World Health Organization) have identified multiple cases of biological threats to agriculture, some of which show signs of intentional introduction:

1) 2004–2007 Cassava Mosaic Virus Spread in East Africa: Though officially considered natural, the rapid spread of mutated strains raised concerns about genetic manipulation or intentional spread (FAO, 2010).

2) 2010 Ug99 Stem Rust (*Puccinia graminis* f. sp. tritici): This pathogen, which originated in Uganda, endangered the world's wheat supplies. Although there is currently insufficient proof, some intelligence reports raised the possibility of engineered dispersal (Singh et al., 2011).

3) 2013 Philippines Coconut Scale Insect Invasion: This was reported as a possible biosecurity breach by the regional office of the FAO because of unexpected outbreaks in plantations under control. The vulnerability of international trade was highlighted but no actor was named.

FAO and WHO recommend the strengthening of phytosanitary border protections, real-time pathogen genomics, and agri-threat forensics units to better attribute such events in the future (FAO & WHO, 2016).

2.3 Case Typologies: Crop, Livestock, and Ecosystem Attacks

Agroterrorism incidents can be classified based on their biological target. Each category involves unique agents, response strategies, and long-term consequences.

2.3.1 Crop-Based Agroterrorism

Target: Staple crops (wheat, rice, maize, cotton).

Agents: Fungi (e.g., rusts), viruses (e.g., TMV), insects (e.g., locusts).

Case Example:

- **Ug99 Wheat Stem Rust:** Threatens 90% of global wheat. Hypothetical links to deliberate spread debated due to resistant gene breakdowns (Singh et al., 2011).
- **Rice Blast Fungus (*Magnaporthe oryzae*):** South Asian outbreaks disrupted food production in the early 2000s.

2.3.2 Livestock-Based Agroterrorism

Target: Cattle, poultry, swine, sheep.

Agents: FMD virus, *Brucella spp.*, African Swine Fever, Rinderpest.

Case Example:

- **2001 FMD in UK:** As discussed, although not confirmed agroterrorism, it demonstrates livestock sector vulnerability.
- **African Swine Fever in China (2018–2019):** Some reports speculated foreign sabotage due to its sudden and vast spread, wiping out 50% of China's pig population (FAO, 2020).

2.3.3 Ecosystem-Based Agroterrorism

Target: Forests, soils, water bodies, pollinators.

Agents: Invasive species, toxic chemicals, biological suppressors.

Case Example:

- **Deliberate introduction of invasive weeds or pests** to disrupt ecosystems (e.g., *Parthenium hysterophorus*).
- **Targeted bee colony collapses** via chemical sabotage have been speculated in politically unstable regions but remain undocumented due to forensic challenges.

Conclusion of Chapter

Through deliberate acts, biosecurity lapses, and possible sabotage in various regions, this chapter proves that agroterrorism is a reality rather than a theoretical idea. Even though full attribution is frequently challenging, the magnitude of the impact these events justify significant scientific, political, and infrastructural attention.

The next chapter will explore the vectors and mechanisms used in these attacks — biological, chemical, and digital — and how each bypasses conventional defense systems.

Chapter 3: Threat Vectors and Mechanisms of Attack

Vartika Singh[1] and Hina Upadhyay[2]*

[1]Ph.D Scholar, School of Bioengineering and Biosciences, Lovely Professional University, Phagwara, Punjab-144001, India

[2]* Associate Professor, Department of Agronomy, School of Agriculture, Lovely Professional University, Phagwara, Punjab-144001, India

***Corresponding author**: hina.18745@lpu.co.in

Modern practices of agriculture are facing convergence of threats from biological, chemical and computational domain. Biological vectors colonize rapidly and outbreak geographically across the farm. Zoonotic pathogens cause devastating livestock epidemics. These vectors are becoming threat for the food security of the country. Over application, misuse and deliberate addition of chemical fertilizer in soil and water cause the damage in crop, soil contamination, water pollution and poisoning to the livestock. Cyber agricultural warfare can sabotage the devices which are integrated with AI for optimized and automated function. Criminal cyber operations can disrupt the productivity, supply chain and economy of country. Enhanced biosecurity, chemical safety, cybersecurity hygiene, diversification of crop and forensic capabilities can mitigate the impact and develop resistance in the ecosystem.

3.1. Biological agent: Threat vector

Biological agents include fungi, bacteria, viruses and zoonotic pathogens which causes significant threat to the crops and livestock because of the diverse mechanism of attack and transmission of the vector. This transmission vector exploits the direct contact, environmental contamination, environmental conditions, vectors and food chains to infect hosts. It causes major economic, health and food security impacts on the population of human being as well and misbalanced the health of ecosystem. Large-scale farming, global trade and close interaction with human and animals increase the risk of rapid disease spread and zoonotic spillover (Gebreyes et al., 2020). Fungi such as Puccinia graminis are mainly spread from the airborne spores which travel long distances and infect leaf surfaces primarily. Bacteria like Xanthomonas are transmitted from water, soil and contaminated equipments and direct plant to plant contact. Entry of bacteria mainly occur through wound and other natural opening of plants. Tobacco mosaic viruses are spread from the mechanical means and plant-to-plant contacts and sometimes from some other vectors. Viruses persist on surfaces for a long time and infect new host when come in contact. Zoonotic pathogens like Brucella and Rinderpest transmit through animal contacts, aerosols, food and water. Livestock work as amplifying host and increases risk of spillover to animals and humans.

3.1.1. Threat vectors and mechanism of invasion in plants

Threat vectors present the routes or agents responsible for introducing and transmitting the pathogens to the host plant species. Pathogen breaches the primary physical barrier such as cuticle and cell wall of plant with the use of mechanical force and enzymatic degradation. Resent research insights show sophisticated coordination between enzymatic arsenals like cutinases, pectinases and cellulases. Application of enormous amount of turgor pressure on the cell wall of specialized structures such as appressoria ruptures the cuticle (de Jong et al., 1997). Effector proteins are secreted simultaneously to suppress the early defenses. Stomata which are also called as breathing pores are essential for the gas exchange in the plants. Pathogen recognizes the chemical cues for locating and invading through the open stomatal pores. In response to the Pathogen associated molecular patterns (PAMPs), plants actively closes their stomata as the stomatal immunity. Pathogen counters stomata closing with their effector proteins and suppresses the closure and forces the reopening of stomata (Melotto et al., 2017). Hydathodes is a water secreting pores at the margin of leaf and during the process of guttation, bacteria like Xanthomonas spp. enter the plant and cause black rot in crucifers. Fungi like Neonectria ditissima cause apple canker through lenticels. Physical damage caused by biotic and abiotic stress creates the entry point for the entry of pathogens inside the cell of plant. Bacteria like Agrobacteriun tumefaciens causes crown gall disease is a major example of pathogen entering in plant through physical damage of plant. Complex defense signaling gets triggers which either exploits or surpasses by the activity of pathogens. Feeding by herbivores often includes the oral secretions containing effector which manipulates the defense system of plant (Chen et al., 2019). Aphids, whiteflies, thrips and leafhoppers work as the vectors for the transmission of viruses, phytoplasma and other bacteria which infect plants. Climate change and global warming is continuously accelerating the distribution and abundance of these vectors in the environment (Whitfield et al., 2015). Some of the root-feeding nematodes and migratory parasites can act as a vector for the fungi and bacteria whereas few of the soil fungi act as a vector for the viruses. Pathogens such as fungi, bacteria, viruses and viroides infect the seeds, tubers, bulbs, grafting and cutting materials and lead to the systematic infection of new plant species in a very new area which is not contaminated. Mites, birds and mammels are also a big contributor in the spread of virus either mechanically or biologically. These methods of vector spread are highly problematic for the global biosecurity. Advanced techniques for the diagnosis at molecular level are crucial for the detection of seed borne pathogens (Bharatbhai, 2019).

3.1.2. Molecular arsenal of attack mechanism

Once the pathogen is inside the host it deploys very sophisticated genetic and biochemical strategies to establish infection in the plant. It also acquires nutrient from the plant and suppress the defense mechanism while increasing the rate of infection.

3.1.2.1. Effector-triggered susceptibility (ETS): Host processes get manipulated by the effector- proteins which are secreted by the pathogens. These effector proteins target key immune signaling hubs hormonal pathway, transcription factor and cellular machinery. It targets and suppresses Pattern-Triggered immunity (PTI) while interfering with the PAMP recognition,

MAPK signaling, kinase signaling, and busting of ROS. Many of the phytohormone signaling such as ABA, JA and SA signaling gets manipulated and alters the expression of gene, proteolysis, autophagy, vesicle trafficking and nutrient leakage in the host plant. Effector-proteins are continuously evolving and fuction inside the nucleus of host cell. Few of the effector-proteins have evolved to target multiple proteins of plant, pathways and plant microbiome (Derevnina et al., 2021; Snelders et al., 2022).

3.1.2.2. Toxin Production: Pathogen secretes compound with low molecular weight to damage the host cell, killing of tissue and disruption of metabolic process which facilitate the colonization in the host cell. Host-Selective Toxins (HSTs) - It affect only specific type of plant genotypes with the corresponding susceptible genes. It is specific in the nature for specific toxins towards the specific plant genotype (Scheffer and Livingston,1984). Non-Host Selective Toxins (NHSTs) – It affects a broad range of host plants, not specific in nature. It causes less effect on the plant as compared to host-selective toxins. Understanding the pathways and gene involved in the biosynthesis of toxic can help to develop resistant breeding and diagnostic mechanisms (Mitchell, 1984).

3.1.2.3. Degradation of Enzyme: Physical barrier such as cellulose, hemicelluloses, pectin and lignin are degraded by wide array of cell wall degrading enzymes and pathogens can access to the nutrients. To avoid the strong defence from the host plants necrotrophic fungi, bacteria and oomycetes have been seen producing fewer amounts of cell wall degrading enzymes. Pathogens seemed to be producing the cocktail of complex and synergistic enzymes which are countered by the enzyme inhibitors of plant.

3.1.2.4. Manipulation of plant hormone: Pathogen alters the synthesis, signaling, metabolism and catabolism of host plant hormone which disturbs defense signaling and development of plant. Jasmonic acid promotes the defense against necrotrophic pathogens. Biotrophs activates Jasmonic acid and suppresses Salicylic acid mediated defense against them. Salicylic acid is the key defense against the biotrophs. Manipulation of plant hormones Auxin, Cytokinins, Gibberellines and Abscisic acid alters plant development, modulate stress, alter defense response and create nutrient sinks. Crosstalk between the hormones is becoming a major battlefield in the manipulation of plant hormone (Chanclud and Morel, 2016).

3.2. Agrochemical contamination in soil and water

Heavy metals, pesticides and excess use of fertilizers are the major source of chemical contamination from the sector of agriculture. It has significant negative impact on the health of soil, quality of water and overall health and stability of ecosystem. Deliberated contamination and misuse of agrochemicals is degrading soil, polluting water, harming non-targeted organisms and causing severe risks to the health of human. Continuous degradation of soil is being seen because of the accumulation of heavy metals, persistent pesticides, herbicides and excess amount of artificial nutrients is disrupting the fertility and structure of soil. It disturbs the microbial diversity and their function which lead to the reduced soil health and lowers the yield of crop (Sarkar et al., 2021; Singh and Singh, 2020; Chaudhary et al., 2023). Chemical contamination cause disturbance in the microbial community affecting soil biochemical processes and nutrient cycling which are essential for the growth of plant (Miller et al., 2020; Chaudhary et al., 2023). Heavy metals and some of the pesticides show long-term persistence in the soil which increases the risk of chronic exposure to organisms and environmental buildup (Sarkar et al., 2021; Singh and Singh, 2020).

3.2.1. Misuse of Agrochemicals and soil water toxins

Improper application and overuse of pesticides, herbicides and fertilizers is leading to run-off and leaching of chemicals and contaminating groundwater with nitrates, phosphates and toxic residues. It is further getting biomagnified in the food chain and contaminating drinking water supplies by point and non-point source of pollutions (Singh and Singh, 2020; Ojo et al., 2024). These chemicals are also causing harm to the non-targeted organisms such as beneficial soil microorganisms which reduce the biodiversity on the environment. It also disrupt the ecological balance with the potential to cause acute and chronic health effects on human and wildlife (Singh and Singh, 2020; Anjaria and Vaghela, 2024). Irrigation with the water containing industrial and tannery effluent put extra toxin and increases salinity in the soil. As a resultant it decreases soil health and productivity of the crop.

3.3. Deliberate severe contamination Indicators

Elevation in the concentration of heavy metals such as lead, arsenic, chromium, nickel etc from the anthropogenic sources are causing serious impact on the ecosystem. Persistent residue of banned pesticides at detectable levels in soil and water are getting biomagnified in the system. It is reducing the diversity of soil microbes and significant shift and decline in the number of beneficial microbes are seen (Sarkar et al., 2021). All of these are together causing abnormality in the soil and plant health, poor crop yield, stunted plant growth and visible symptoms of toxicity in plants. Deterioration in the quality of water nearby water bodies are seen because of the increased nitrate, phosphate and other toxicant concentration (Miller et al., 2020).

3.4. Cyber warfare in Agriculture

Global and rapid adaptation of AI sensors, IoT, and data-driven tools are being continuously integrated in the field of agriculture for real-time insights and promotes smart farming. It has greatly increased the productivity but on the other hand introduced significant vulnerabilities of cyber warfare. Cyber-attacks which can sabotage these systems can harm the critical operations of irrigation, pesticide use and fertilizer application which can cause devastating effect on the food security and supply chain. Smart-farming mechanisms are integrated with the IoT tools and sensors are interconnected devices for monitoring and automated performances. Attackers can exploit these tools which have weak security in their devices to disrupt the flow of data to manipulate the reading from the sensors. By manipulating the sensor readings of automated equipments and taking control of automated equipments can lead to incorrect irrigation and fertilizer application. It can further lead to the reduced yield in the crop and may damage the crop completely (Alahmadi et al., 2020; Gupta et al., 2020; Rudrakar and Rughani, 2023). Falsification in data collection, interpretation and sabotage in the system can lead in the manipulation of predictive analysis. Cybercriminals can sabotage and falsify the data which are obtained from the AI based sensors and tamper them with the control systems. It can cause over- or under-watering in the field, over application or under application of fertilizer and may halt the operation completely. These kinds of sabotages in the field can result in significant economic and environmental losses (Gupta et al., 2020; Rudrakar & Rughani, 2023). Disconnection of sensor from device because of Wi-Fi deauthentication can prevent real-time monitoring and control of field especially during critical period such as harvesting (Sontowski et al., 2020). Side-channels and advanced attacks are the emerging threat which includes side-channel attacks which exploits indirect leak of information from the devices and compromises the integrity of system (Alahmadi et al., 2020).

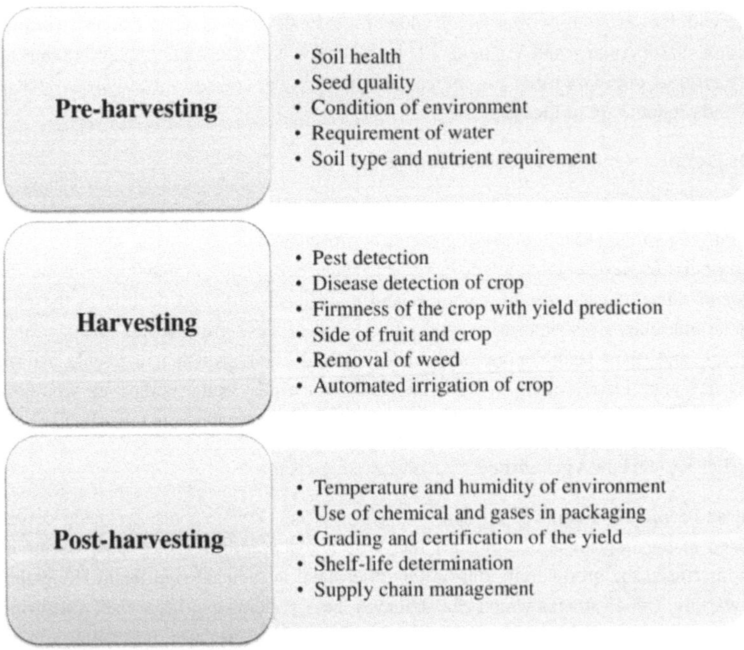

Fig 1: Phases for the integration AI in the field of Agriculture

3.4.1. Consequences and mitigation measures of cyber warfare in agriculture

Falsification of data causes severe impact such as failure of crop, waste of resources and disruption of food supply chain. Failure of system and sabotage of equipment can lead to the halt in operation for very long period of time. Sometimes network attacks cause loss of monitoring and control resulting in delayed response for making decisions. Theft of data and loss of sensitive information cause the manipulation in market resulting in disturbance in supply chain. Advanced system of intrusion detection by machine learning and deep learning can help in identification and detection and provide real-time response. It offers high accuracy in detection of threat and helps in cyber threat intelligence and detection (Aldhyani & Alkahtani, 2023). Regular update on system with strong credentials and segmented networks are some of the essential practices which can prevent from cyberattacks. For diverting attackers, deception technologies can help in decoying and trapping.

Conclusion

Biological agents attack crops and livestock through various mechanisms. It is caused by vectors, mechanical and biological pathways. Making rapid response system and cross sector collaboration can help in effective control and prevention of disease. Chemical contamination because of the overuse of agrochemicals and deliberate pollution from anthropogenic sources are degrading soil and water health and impacting environment and human health. Important indicator of the pollution are elevated level of toxins, persistent residue, reduced biodiversity. Sustainable agricultural practices, monitoring of the level of toxins released from the source and remediation of these toxins at standard level are some of the essentials to protect soil and water from damage. Farming system with integrated AI technologies are highly vulnerable for the cyber warfare with attacks on sensors with AI, IoT and control systems causing serious risk to farm operations and food security. Proactive measure in the field of cyber security with advance detection system and preparedness can help in safeguarding agriculture from these evolving threats.

Chapter 4: Agricultural Vulnerability Assessment: Indian Context

Vartika Singh[1] and Hina Upadhyay[2]*

[1]Ph.D Scholar, School of Bioengineering and Biosciences, Lovely Professional University, Phagwara, Punjab-144001, India

[2]* Associate Professor, Department of Agronomy, School of Agriculture, Lovely Professional University, Phagwara, Punjab-144001, India

***Corresponding author**: hina.18745@lpu.co.in

Indian agriculture sector is facing intensifying vulnerabilities because of the climate change, resources pressure and globalization. Agriculture is the bedrock for the economy and food security of the country. Prevalence of major pests and diseases are being exacerbated by the climate change and monocropping, causes higher loss in high-density areas. Supply chain of seeds are maintained by central and state institutions and at large extent private players are also playing major role in maintaining seed supply chain. Integrating digital infrastructure in agriculture sector can help in the penetration of information in rural areas and fill the gap of digital literacy. Conceptualizing a Bio-fragility Index for the sector of Agriculture can capture biological risks, economics and infrastructure sensitivities which can cause vulnerabilities. Understanding Bio-fragility Index can help in developing adaption and mitigation strategies.

4.1. Introduction

Agricultural vulnerability Assessment (AVA) is important for understanding the critical process and susceptibility of the country's vast and diverse agricultural system towards various stressors like climate change, economic shift, market volatility and degradation of environment Varadan and Kumar, 2015). This help in understanding the potential negative impacts on crop yield, production from livestock, economic growth of farmers and overall food security of the global population. AVA can help in determining the magnitude of stressors such as increased frequency of droughts, floods, unseasonal rain, heatwave and cyclones in the eastern coast of the country. Floods majorly affect major regions of Assam and Bihar; heatwave cause severe impact in the region of Indo-Gangetic Plains whereas unseasonal rain cause crop damage in the rabi season crops. Gradual rise in the temperature because of climate change is affecting crop phenology in the wheat crop of state Punjab and Haryana. Variability in the rainfall patterns, rise in the sea-level and increased salinity in the coastal areas like Sundarbans are causing decline in the fertility of soil. Non-climatic stressors such as fluctuation in the market prices cause increase in the input cause. Pest and disease outbreak, degradation of land, soil erosion, salinity in soil and depletion in the level of groundwater are becoming major non-climatic stressors. Challenges which are being faced in AVA are data gaps, mismatch scale, dynamic complexity, local knowledge integration and uncertainty of future of long-term climate impacts in upcoming years.

4.1.1. Sensitivity towards the stressors

The degree at which agriculture sector will be affected is completely dependent on the sensitivity. Different crop species faces different level of sensitivity towards different kind of stressors. Various type of crop shows different level of vulnerability towards water stress, terminal heat, hailstorm and phenological stages. Crop productivity is also dependent on resources such as irrigation and fertilizer. Depletion in the resources cause degradation of soil, fragment landholdings and deplete aquifers. Dependency of small farmers on agriculture for income and subsidies is limiting their savings and increasing indebtedness and causing sensitivity in generating livelihood (Cheng et al., 2024).

4.1.2. Capability of adaptation

To adjust and cope with the consequences of moderate potential damage there is a requirement to develop adaptive capability at farmers, community and institution level. At farm-level access of irrigation system can be provided through canal, groundwater and micro-irrigation systems which can help in growing crop in the drought prominent agricultural lands. Developing drought, heat and flood resistant seeds through genetic engineering provide chances of diversification in the crop and increase the yield. Developing mitigation strategies and adaptive capability are very helpful in developing financial resources as well as knowledge and skills. At community level social networks and cooperative institutions are being developed to provide access of resources to all the sector of community with a collaborative action. At institution and system level, early warning systems should be integrated with the AI technologies to provide predictive analysis. Effective early warning systems, crop insurance scheme like PMFBY, access to credit for farmers, agricultural extension services, providing market infrastructure, established supply chain, disaster relief and government policies such as NAPCC, SAPCCs and NICRA are some of the adaptive methods for mitigating the impact of vulnerabilities.

4.2. Important drivers for Agricultural vulnerabilities in India

Most of the seasonal crops are dependent on the monsoon in India. High dependency and erratic pattern of monsoon are directly impacting most of the kharif crop of India as well as the groundwater recharge. Over half of the agricultural land of country lacks assured irrigation system and make it highly susceptible to variable rainfall. Farmers with small landholdings limiting economies, investment capabilitiės and risks the ability of absorption. Poverty and indebtedness limit the ability of farmers to invest in the adaptive and mitigation measures which can help them to recover from losses. Vulnerabilities are causing major degradation of natural resources such as soil erosion, decline of soil organic carbon, declining groundwater table and loss of the natural flora and fauna from the region. These all factors are together contributing in reducing the resilience in the ecosystem. Because of the regional disparities vulnerabilities varies drastically across different agro-climatic zones. Dryland of Rajasthan, floodplains of Bihar and coastal deltas face different varies and it varies drastically from each region to another.

4.2.1. Assessment methods in India

Indicator-based Approaches are being used by combining biophysical parameters such as soil, slope, variable rainfall and socio-economic parameters like literacy, irrigation access, and landholding size are major indicators into composite indices. This is majorly done at the district level. Simulating crop yield and modeling climate crop under various climatic conditions can help in identification of crops and regions using DSSAT and APSIM models. Major participation from rural communities and engaging farmers as well as local communities are helping in understanding perceived vulnerabilities, local adaptation strategies and mitigation methods. Monitoring land use, health of vegetation, soil moisture analysis and extent of natural calamities are being provided in real-time through remote sensing and GIS. Household surveys for collecting data on the basis of income sources, assets, losses experienced earlier and employed adaptation strategies.

2.2. Regional Hotspots of vulnerabilities in India

Parts of Rajasthan, Madhya Pradesh, Maharashtra, Gujarat, Karnataka, Telangana, Andhra Pradesh are the dryland and highly sensitive to droughts in these rainfed regions (Kumar et al., 2024). Eastern coaster region of Odisha, Andhra Pradesh, West Bengal and Tamil Nadu are

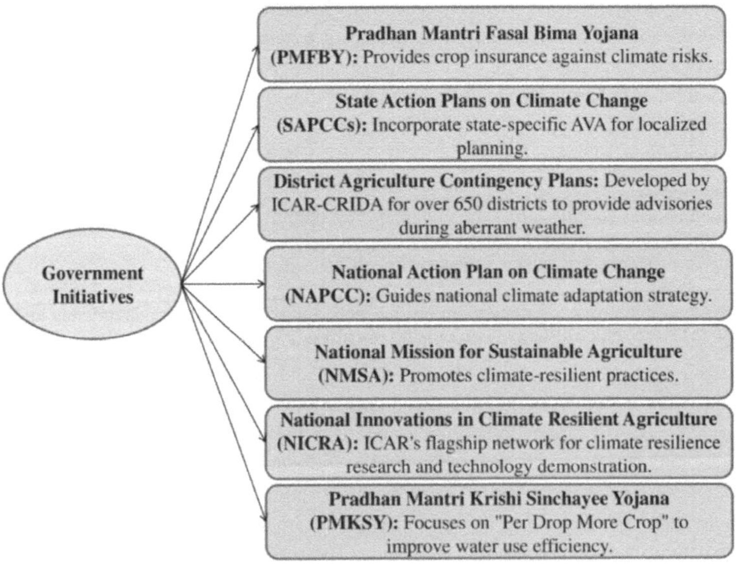

Fig 2: Policy relevance and Government initiatives

vulnerable to cyclones, ingress of salinity and rise of the sea-level (Senapati and Das, 2024). Regions of Assam, Bihar, Eastern Uttar Pradesh and some regions of West Bengal are prone to flood. It also faces major damage of crop and infrastructure. Himalayan foothills of Uttarakhand and Himachal Pradesh are very much vulnerable to landslides. Crop of this region get affected by the changing pattern of snowfall and impact of glacier melt. Indo-gangetic Plains are very productive region and produce high yield of wheat but increased heat stress in the wheat crop are causing depletion in the groundwater level and poses significant threat.

4.3. Analysis of biosecurity in Agriculture

In Indian agriculture, biosecurity encompasses the policies, strategies and practices. It is aimed for the prevention, introduction, establishment and spread of disease, pest and invasive species which can threaten the productivity of agriculture as well as damages food security, biodiversity, trade and livelihood of rural population.

1) Lump Skin Disease: It was a devastating outbreak of a viral disease which has affected cattles in Asia. It affected millions of cattle and caused high morbidity which has significantly increased the rate of mortality. LSD has shown reduction in milk production and caused economic losses which are estimated to billions of dollars. Implication of biosecurity in livestock disease Surveillance, transparency in reporting, availability of vaccine, deployment speed of vaccine, controlled cross border movement and awareness in farmers can cover up the critical weaknesses (Kumar et al., 2021). Massive emergency vaccination was done using goat pox vaccine and which was further replaced by indigenous Lumpi-ProVaclnd vaccine which was developed by ICAR. More focuse was done on containment, movement and carcass disposal protocols.

2) Avian Influenza (Bird Flu) Recurrence: It is a seasonal outbreak of Highly Pathogenic Avian Influenza (HPAI) particularly strain H5N1 and H5N8 occurs in the poultry farms both at commercial and backyard level in the states of Kerala, Maharashtra, Explores, Bihar and Uttar Pradesh almost annually. Outbreak of this disease leads to the massive culling, trade restrictions and economic alginate to the farmers. This emphasizes the threat of zoonotic diseases and the challenge of controlling the spread of virus by migratory birds (Memish et al., 2024). Strengthening farm-level biosecurity by Sanitation, isolation and wild bird deterrence can reduce the chances of contamination when they are implemented evenly. Standard procol for controlling the disease are culling within the infected zones, restriction of movement, surveillance in surrounding area and disinfection.

3) Fall Armyworm (FAW) Persistence: *Spodoptera fugiperda* which is also called as FAW has become a major established invasive pest for maize and other crops in the country in recent years. It demonstrates vulnerabilities to invasive species introduction by trade and travel. Cross border spread within the southern Asian region remains a concern. Currently these challenges which are being faced by the researches are the capability of pest managing resistance to insecticides and developing new variants with more survivability and resistance. ICAR and State Agricultural Universities are continuously extending research on biological control agents, pheromone traps, resistant hybrid crops and training farmers for integrated pest management. It is also emphasizing on early detection and control systems.

4.3.1. Border Vigilance for Emerging Threats

Continuous Vigilance against the wheat blast, which was first detected in the border region of Bangladesh was contained by strict quarantine and surveillance in the border States such as West Bengal, Bihar and regions of Jharkhand. Continuous researches to delelop resistant varieties are currently going on. African Swine Fever (ASF) is yet not reported from India but still it poses a severe threat to piggery sector. The key recent biosecurity activities to prevent the entry of this disease in Indian soil are heightened security surveillance in north-east especially, surveillance at airport and seaport for illegal pork imports and awareness campaigns against the disease.

4.4. Key biosecurity challenges and Policy, Infrastructure development

With inadequate funding, insufficient trained personnel like pathologist, entomologists, plant pathologist, veterinary scientist, doctors and capability to diagnose the disease are very constrain at the grassroots level. As India is a very vast country with diverse landscape system so monitoring and controlling pest and disease spread across million of small and marginals farms become very difficult to understand and control. National Digital Livestock Mission (NDLM) was launched to create a digital architecture for identification, traceability, disease and health record management. The aim of NDLM was to significantly improve disease Surveillance, outbreak response and control the movement to enhance biosecurity for long term. Ongoing efforts of strengthening the labs and upgrading National Animal Disease Referral Expert System (NADRES) network and National Institute of High Security Animal Disease can help in better understanding and restraining the contamination which can reduce economic, ecosystem and health damage. Growing recognition and policy discussion can help in the integration and management of human, animal and environmental health which can help in tackling zoonoses like Anthrax, Avian flu and potential spillover. Establishing One Health Mission at National level can be a key step to focus on one health approach of country. It can also help with the detection and containment of the contamination.

4.5. Seed supply chains, Mandis and Cold Storage in India

To reduce post-harvest losses, improve market efficiency and ensure accessibility of inputs, agricultural infrastructure is a necessity. Seed supply chain at national level is maintained by ICAR (Indian Council of Agricultural Research) institutes, National Seeds Corporation (NSC) and SFCI (State Farms Corporation of India). States institutes such as SSCS (State Seed Corporations), SAUs (State Agricultural Universities) and private sector also plays defining role in maintaining seed infrastructure. Bayer, Syngenta, UPL and Advanta are some of the major regional player of private sector in maintaining the seed supply chain Infrastructure. With the aim for preventing spurious seeds, traceability and streamline licensing, eSeedChain was implemented under National Mission on Agriculture Extension and Technology (NMAET). Government is continuously developing infrastructure and increasing capacity of testing and certification. States such as Telangana, Maharashtra and Karnataka are modernizing SSC infrastructure with the funding from state and center.

4.5.1. Mandi and cold storage Infrastructure

North-East states have minimum coverage of mandis whereas states like Punjab, Haryana, Maharashtra, Madhya Pradesh, Karnataka and Gujarat have a denser network of Mandis. Currently mandis are being integrated electronically with the platforms which can facilitate online bidding, payment system and dashboards. Uttar Pradesh, West Bengal, Punjab, Gujarat and Maharashtra have significant share of cold storage infrastructure. In Uttar Pradesh, the potato cultivating region such as Varanasi, Agra and Meerut have the major national capacity of cold storage.

4.6. National Bio-Economic Fragility Index

The bio-economic fragility implicitly in India is measured by converging indexes of climate, socio-economic risks and biosecurity. Recent natural calamities show vulnerabilities in high-density agricultural zones like Indo-Gangetic Plains and coastal regions. Integrating data from National Disaster Risk Index (NDRI), Agriculture Vulnerability to Climate Change (MoES) and Livestock Vulnerability Index (LVI) can help in understanding National Bio-Economic Fragility Index. This can help in guiding investment, developing resilient seeds and safety nets for adaption and mitigation according to the changes.

Conclusion

AVA is indispensable for safeguarding the livelihood of millions of farmer's and food security in the face of increasing climate risks and presence of other stressors. Assessment of agricultural vulnerabilities is important for safeguarding the food security of global population. It helps in prioritizing investments, climate resilient varieties, water management and diversification of crops. Currently India is facing significant biosecurity challenge in agriculture because of the evolving climatic conditions. Research laboratories are actively responding through vaccination drives, pest management research, digital initiatives and policy shift towards one health. To modernize seed chains, mandis and cold storages, India is making significant scheme-driven investment. Bio-Economic Fragility Index can make a significant change in assesment of risk across the sector.

Chapter 5: Socioeconomic and Food Security Implications of Agroterrorism

Dibyendu Nayak[1*] and Furquan Khalid[2]

[1*] School of Agriculture, Lovely Professional University, Phagwara, Punjab-144001, India

[2]School of Agriculture, Lovely Professional University, Phagwara, Punjab-144001, India

***Corresponding author**: dibyendunayak05@gmail.com

Beyond the immediate ecological or biological harm, agroterrorism has far-reaching effects because it intentionally disrupts agricultural systems. An important layer of vulnerability can be seen by the socioeconomic implications, which can show up as price volatility, food insecurity, rural distress, and even national trade and nutrition crises. The repercussions of agroterrorism on rural society and the larger food economy are examined in this chapter.

5.1 Multiplier Effect on Food Prices and Inflation

Agroterrorism introduces supply-side shocks by disrupting crop production, livestock availability, and agri-logistics. These shocks have a non-linear multiplier effect on the entire food value chain.

5.1.1 Price Volatility and Consumer Inflation

- Disruption of key staples (e.g., wheat, rice, pulses, vegetables) causes immediate inflationary spikes.
- Targeted crop attacks, such as locusts in Rajasthan or rice blast in Odisha, would decrease local supply and increase reliance on imports or interstate transportation, which would raise market prices.
- According to RBI inflation data, food articles constitute 45.86% of the Consumer Price Index (CPI) in India, means agricultural disruption directly impacts inflation (RBI, 2023).

5.1.2 Supply Chain Disruptions

- Agroterror attacks generally target weak points in the supply chain—such as food processing hubs or cold storage facilities.
- High waste rates for perishable goods cause hoarding, unusual price increases, and artificial scarcity.

5.2 Regional Food Insecurity and the Role of NFSA/PDS

Agroterrorism disproportionately affects vulnerable populations who rely on public food systems.

5.2.1 NFSA & Targeted Vulnerability

- The National Food Security Act (NFSA), 2013, covers 75% of the rural population and 50% of the urban population.
- A disruption in PDS-linked crops (e.g., rice, wheat) due to agroterror can paralyze TPDS (Targeted Public Distribution System) functionality.
- If attacks directly affected buffer stock systems under FCI management, especially in remote and tribal areas, PDS dependability would be compromised.

5.2.2 Nutritional Consequences

- FAO estimates that any 10% drop in staple grain production in low-income countries can cause a 15–20% rise in childhood malnutrition.
- India, which relies heavily on subsidized grains, would see spikes in regional undernutrition, especially in aspirational districts.

5.3 Impact on Rural Livelihoods and Mental Health

5.3.1 Rural Employment and Livelihood Collapse

- Agriculture provides direct employment to over 45% of India's population (MoAFW, 2022).
- By using disease vectors, livestock poisoning, or pest sabotage, agroterrorism has the potential to completely destroy seasonal incomes.
- Casual laborers and marginal farmers, particularly in monoculture areas (such as the cotton belt in Vidarbha or tea estates in North Bengal), experience total economic paralysis.

5.3.2 NCRB Data on Farmer Suicides and Distress

According to the National Crime Records Bureau (NCRB):

- In India, 11,290 farmers and agricultural workers died by suicide in 2022. This was 7.2% of all suicides in the country (NCRB, 2023).
- The highest incidence was reported in Maharashtra, Telangana, and Karnataka, primarily due to crop failure and financial difficulties.
- Agroterrorism, if it induces widespread crop losses or livestock culling, can amplify this mental health burden.

5.3.3 Psychological Insecurity

- A climate of fear and unstability brought on by the expectation of more attacks hinders agri-investments and sowing decisions.\

- The psychological effects are increased by a lack of trust in government or insurance compensation (PMFBY data indicates that less than 40% of claims are settled in some states).

5.4 Cross-Sectoral Impacts: Trade, Nutrition, and Ecosystem

5.4.1 National and International Trade Disruptions

India is the world's largest exporter of Basmati rice and spices. Any agroterror event targeting these commodities can trigger global trade restrictions, such as:

- EU restrictions on Indian chillies in 2017 (fungal toxin scare).
- Because of an outbreak of the Nipah virus, the UAE has stopped importing fresh fruits and vegetables from Kerala, India. According to the Times of India, TRT Global, and Reuters, this ban came into effect on May 29, 2018.

Loss of export credibility directly reduces foreign exchange earnings and depresses farmer earnings.

5.4.2 Nutrition Chain Breakdown

- Targeting pulses, oilseeds, or livestock directly affects protein availability.
- WHO already warns that protein-energy malnutrition increases significantly with even minor disruptions in animal-based food systems.
- According to NFHS-5, 40% of Indian children under the age of five are already underweight, and agroterrorism may make the country's malnutrition statistics worse.

5.4.3 Long-Term Ecological Consequences

- Biological attacks (like invasive weed dispersal or engineered fungi) create persistent soil toxicity.
- Agrochemicals used in countermeasures have the potential to harm ecosystems by affecting biodiversity, pollinators, and water bodies.
- As an example, using paraquat and chemical burnouts to eradicate invasive pests frequently results in secondary ecological harm that impacts fisheries and wildlife.

Conclusion of Chapter

Agroterrorism, while often perceived as a sectoral threat, is in reality a national crisis multiplier. Its ripple effects extend across economics, food access, nutrition, employment, mental health, and ecological stability. The synergistic damage it causes demands integrated policies that bridge agriculture, public health, security, and social welfare.

Chapter 6: Risk Management and International Frameworks

Sounak Chakraborty*

*School of Agriculture, Lovely Professional University, Phagwara (Punjab), India-144411

*Corresponding author: sounak291@gmail.com

Agroterrorism takes advantage of weaknesses in biological systems, agricultural ecology, and the food supply chain to undermine traditional defenses. National preparedness is not enough because pests, diseases, and genetically modified threats are transboundary. In this chapter, the layered architecture of agroterrorism risk management is examined in relation to international frameworks, treaty obligations, and scientific monitoring systems. It discusses the International Plant Protection Convention (IPPC), the United Nations Biological Weapons Convention (BWC), and new technologies for early detection and real-time response.

6.1 The UN Biological Weapons Convention (BWC): Legal Foundation for Agro-Biosecurity

6.1.1 Historical Context and Provisions

The Biological Weapons Convention (BWC) was signed in 1972 and came into force in 1975 as the world's first multilateral treaty to ban the use and development of biological weapons. As of 2024, the Convention has 184 States Parties.

The core obligation under Article I prohibits:
"Microbial or other biological agents, or toxins, whatever their origin or method of production... for purposes other than prophylactic, protective or other peaceful purposes."

This broad phrasing allows inclusion of agricultural pathogens, toxins harmful to crops or livestock, and genetically engineered bio-agents targeting food security infrastructure.

6.1.2 Relevance to Agroterrorism

While the BWC primarily addresses threats to human health, its scope implicitly covers plant, animal, and ecosystem-based bioterrorism, provided they are used for hostile purposes. Agroterrorism fits within the BWC's legal scope because:

- It involves intentional deployment of biological agents (e.g., fungal blight, anthrax spores) against agriculture.
- It severely impairs social cohesiveness, economies, and food production, causing widespread societal disruption.
- Such acts can be perpetrated by non-state actors, using tools of warfare traditionally outside the scope of conventional arms control.

6.1.3 Institutional Limitations

Despite its comprehensive legal scope, the BWC has critical limitations:

- **Lack of verification mechanisms:** Unlike the Chemical Weapons Convention (CWC), the BWC has no system of on-site inspections or data declarations.
- **Under-resourcing of agriculture-specific threats:** BWC Review Conferences have primarily emphasized human biosecurity, with limited discussion of agricultural and food chain vulnerabilities.
- **Ambiguity in attribution:** Agroterrorism often overlaps with natural outbreaks or climate-induced pathogen shifts, complicating legal enforcement under BWC.

6.1.4 Strategic Recommendations

To better integrate agroterrorism in the BWC framework:

- Establish a sub-protocol or annex focusing specifically on agricultural and environmental bio-agents.
- Mandate dual-use biotechnology reporting for agricultural research with potential misuse risk.
- Encourage integration between the BWC Implementation Support Unit (ISU) and international plant and animal health organizations (FAO, OIE, IPPC).

6.2 The International Plant Protection Convention (IPPC): A Global Shield for Plant Health

6.2.1 Overview and Governance

The IPPC is a legally binding agreement that was created in 1951 and is hosted by the FAO. To date, 184 parties have signed on it. Its objective is to prevent the introduction and spread of pests that affect plants and plant-derived products while promoting safe trade.

The IPPC operates through:

- International Standards for Phytosanitary Measures (ISPMs).
- Global surveillance, quarantine, and inspection protocols.
- Capacity building via Regional Plant Protection Organizations (RPPOs).

6.2.2 Application to Agroterrorism

Despite not being a counterterrorism organization, the IPPC performs a de facto security function by:

- Enabling early detection and rapid containment of exotic and intentionally introduced pests.

- Providing a legal framework for national quarantine actions without violating WTO trade laws.
- Offering standardized diagnostic and emergency protocols, which can be rapidly adapted for deliberate pathogen release scenarios.

For example, ISPM No. 9 outlines procedures for pest eradication, including stakeholder engagement, which can be adapted for high-risk agro-bio events.

6.2.3 National Implementation: India's NPPO

India's National Plant Protection Organization (NPPO) under the Directorate of Plant Protection (Ministry of Agriculture) enforces IPPC standards through:

- Plant Quarantine (Regulation of Import into India) Order, 2003
- Pest Risk Analysis (PRA) before introducing new crops or technologies
- National pest surveillance networks covering key crops like wheat (rust), cotton (bollworm), and rice (blast)

6.3 Early Detection and Rapid Response Systems (EDRRs)

6.3.1 Concept and Principles

EDRRs are proactive defense systems that emphasize:

- Timely identification of abnormal plant health patterns or pest populations
- Geospatial modeling for pathogen spread prediction
- Mobilization of control teams and resource allocation within 24–72 hours of detection

Unlike passive reporting systems, EDRRs are intelligence-driven, using data fusion from satellites, AI models, meteorological records, and ground truthing.

6.3.2 International Case Studies

- **United States: NPDN and CAPS**
  The **National Plant Diagnostic Network (NPDN)** and **Cooperative Agricultural Pest Survey (CAPS)** under **USDA-APHIS** form the backbone of the U.S. EDRR framework.

- **Europe: EUROPHYT & TRACES-NT**
  The **EUROPHYT** platform monitors pest interceptions at ports of entry and shares data in real time across the EU.

- **India: ICAR-led Disease Surveillance Networks**
  The Indian Council of Agricultural Research (ICAR) has developed **geo-tagged**

surveillance models for wheat rusts, blast diseases, and mosaic viruses, linked to weather forecasting.

6.4 Real-Time Phytosanitary Monitoring Systems

6.4.1 Role of Remote Sensing and Digital Diagnostics

Modern phytosanitary surveillance uses remote sensing, hyperspectral imaging, machine learning, and internet-enabled biosensors.

- **Drones** identify crop anomalies by detecting temperature differentials and chlorophyll reflectance.
- **AI models** can classify images of infected crops and predict disease progression.
- **Sensor networks** embedded in fields can continuously monitor temperature, moisture, and airborne spores.

6.4.2 Institutional Platforms and Tools

Table 2: Platforms, Tools and Relevance to Agroterrorism

Platform	***Functionality***	***Relevance to Agroterrorism***
PlantwisePlus (CABI)	Global pest diagnosis and treatment database	Enables rapid identification of novel bio-agents
EPPO Global Database	Monitors quarantine pests and regulated species	Identifies cross-border threats and patterns
FRACTAL Model (EU)	Predictive analysis of plant disease spread	Useful for modeling impact zones in agroterror events
eLocust3 (FAO)	Mobile-based desert locust surveillance	Template for future agro-bio surveillance tools

Conclusion of Chapter

Legal tools, scientific diagnostics, and real-time intelligence coordination are necessary for the prevention and mitigation of agroterrorism. Although the BWC offers a fundamental legal framework, it needs to be strengthened by EDRR technologies and supplemented by phytosanitary enforcement under the IPPC. Building compatible networks of biosecurity stakeholders—integrating academic labs, international organizations, border security, and agriculture ministries—is the way of the future.

Chapter 7: Institutional Responses and Scientific Preparedness in India

Dibyendu Nayak[1*] and Anindya Sanyal[2]

[1*] School of Agriculture, Lovely Professional University, Phagwara, Punjab-144001, India

[2]School of Agriculture, Lovely Professional University, Phagwara, Punjab-144001, India

***Corresponding author**: dibyendunayak05@gmail.com

7.1 Introduction

One of the biggest agrarian economies in the world, India is still at risk from agroterrorism attacks that take advantage of the biosecurity flaws in its agricultural and food systems. Although we have established a multi-tiered institutional architecture for food safety, disaster management, and agricultural development, we are still working to be ready for intentional biological events in the agricultural sector. This chapter assesses the state of scientific infrastructure, current regulatory frameworks, and the function of important national agencies in reducing the threat of agroterrorism and managing such events.

7.2 Role of Core Institutions

7.2.1 National Disaster Management Authority (NDMA)

NDMA, established under the Disaster Management Act, 2005, is India's apex body for disaster risk reduction and management. While NDMA has comprehensive guidelines on biological disasters, agroterrorism is yet to be recognized as a standalone threat. However, NDMA supports state-level agricultural contingency planning and epidemic protocols through coordination with the Ministry of Agriculture and Farmers' Welfare. Current efforts primarily focus on zoonotic outbreaks and large-scale pest invasions (NDMA, 2016).

7.2.2 Indian Council of Agricultural Research (ICAR)

ICAR oversees a vast network of 74 agricultural universities and 113 institutes, including Bureaus and National Research Centers (NRCs) that focus on climate resilience, animal health, plant pathology, and biosafety. Its main divisions, the National Bureau of Plant Genetic Resources (NBPGR) and the National Institute of High-Security Animal Diseases (NIHSAD), provide specialized infrastructure for diagnostics and containment. Although it does not have a central coordination cell dedicated to the detection of biocrimes or agroterrorists, ICAR plays a significant role in the development of resistant crop varieties, early detection tools, and contingency plans.

7.2.3 Food Safety and Standards Authority of India (FSSAI)

FSSAI, while primarily focused on consumer-end food safety and adulteration control, contributes indirectly through its surveillance of microbial food hazards. It has developed a robust network of food testing laboratories but does not currently have a mandate to address pre-harvest biological threats such as deliberate pathogen exposure to crops or livestock.

7.2.4 Defence Research and Development Organisation (DRDO)

In India's biodefense environment, DRDO is essential. Counter-Biological Warfare research and development is carried out by the Institute of Nuclear Medicine and Allied Sciences (INMAS) and the Defence Research and Development Establishment (DRDE). They still play a relatively small role in agricultural biosecurity, though, and have few connections to civilian organizations like NDMA or ICAR. India's capacity to implement a comprehensive agroterrorism response is weakened by this fragmented strategy.

7.3 Existing Protocols and Legal Instruments

7.3.1 Plant Quarantine (Regulation of Import into India) Order, 2003

This order, issued under the **Destructive Insects and Pests Act (1914)**, governs the import of plants and plant materials to prevent the entry of invasive pests or pathogens. While it is **India's primary phytosanitary framework**, it was not designed with intentional bio-threats in mind. The lack of digital surveillance integration, risk modeling tools, and real-time genomic diagnostics limits its utility in a post-9/11 bioterrorism-aware era.

7.3.2 Animal Quarantine and Certification Services (AQCS)

The **Department of Animal Husbandry and Dairying** oversees **AQCS**, which keeps an eye on livestock and animal products. But historically, the system has prioritized routine checks over complex forensic detection of pathogens that have been genetically modified or grown in a lab.

7.4 Deficiencies in National Contingency Planning

- **Lack of a Central Agro-Biosecurity Authority:** India does not currently have a centralized authority that focuses on agricultural bio-crimes, deliberate pest/pathogen release, or coordinated agro-defense.
- **Inter-Agency Disconnection:** Important organizations like ICAR, DRDO, NDMA, and FSSAI operate independently, which leads to fragmented response systems and communication breakdowns in early warning.
- **Limited Training in Agroforensics**: Law enforcement and agricultural officers are rarely trained in detecting or managing deliberate biological attacks on crops or livestock.
- **Low Priority in National Security Doctrine:** The lack of clear inclusion of agroterrorism in national security threats restricts funding and research focus.

7.5 Scientific Infrastructure and R&D Initiatives

7.5.1 Krishi Vigyan Kendras (KVKs)

KVKs function as grassroots agricultural knowledge and extension hubs. While they are instrumental in pest outbreak monitoring and farmer training, their capacity to handle agroterrorist events is non-existent. Introducing bio-threat modules and plant protection drills can help transform KVKs into early-warning nodes.

7.5.2 Agricultural Technology Management Agency (ATMA)

ATMA facilitates decentralized agricultural planning and farmer engagement. It has untapped potential to serve as a surveillance and communication channel for community-based agro-biosecurity. Integrating bio-threat awareness in ATMA's district-level action plans could bridge the gap between scientific research and field-level resilience.

7.5.3 Indian Agricultural Statistics Research Institute (IASRI)

IASRI has pioneered the use of machine learning and AI for crop prediction. These models can be adapted to develop anomaly detection systems for crop failure caused by bio-threats, integrating weather, pest, and soil health data with satellite imagery and remote sensing.

7.6 Recommendations for Institutional Strengthening

- Establish a **National Agro-Biosecurity Coordination Centre (NABCC)** to unify civilian and defense agro-biosecurity research and response.
- Mandate periodic agroterrorism simulations and inter-agency drills involving NDMA, ICAR, DRDO, and state agriculture departments.
- Upgrade Plant and Animal Quarantine facilities with **next-gen molecular diagnostics**, **AI-driven risk prediction**, and **blockchain traceability**.
- This includes **Agroterrorism Preparedness** in the national disaster education curriculum and state agriculture university syllabi.

7.7 Conclusion

India's institutional architecture for agricultural and biological resilience is strong in order but limited in integration, enforcement, and scientific innovation when it comes to agroterrorism. Strengthening cross-sectoral linkages, creating a unified bio-threat response strategy, and investing in agro-forensic science are not optional in an era where food systems are increasingly being viewed as soft targets for disruption. A scientifically anchored, policy-supported, and community-inclusive approach is urgently needed to safeguard India's bio-economy against covert and deliberate biological threats.

Chapter 8: Policy Recommendations and Strategic Roadmap

Dibyendu Nayak[1*] and Anindya Sanyal[2]

[1*] School of Agriculture, Lovely Professional University, Phagwara, Punjab-144001, India

[2]School of Agriculture, Lovely Professional University, Phagwara, Punjab-144001, India

***Corresponding author**: dibyendunayak05@gmail.com

Agroterrorism threatens public health, biodiversity, national security, and economic stability. To effectively defend against deliberate biological attacks on crops and livestock, India needs to put in place a multi-layered, integrated policy framework. A comprehensive roadmap based on institutional reform, community engagement, education, funding, implementation, surveillance infrastructure, and international cooperation is provided in this chapter.

8.1 National Agrosecurity Mission (NASM)

8.1.1 Why NASM?

Agricultural biothreats have the potential to be life-threatening, but they are not yet specifically addressed in India's national security and disaster management frameworks. A dedicated **National Agrosecurity Mission (NASM)** under the **Ministry of Agriculture & Farmers' Welfare** is recommended to ensure central coordination across:

- **NDMA** (emergency response)
- **ICAR** (agricultural diagnostics & research)
- **FSSAI** (food safety governance)
- **DRDO** (biodefense technology)
- **NPPO** (phytosanitary protection)
- State agriculture and veterinary departments

NASM would bridge institutional gaps by creating a unified, mission-oriented approach to agro-biosecurity threats.

8.1.2 Mission Objectives

1. Build a centralized governance structure, including a Steering Council comprising senior officials from **NDMA, ICAR, DRDO, FSSAI, NPPO**, and state agriculture departments.
2. Create a dedicated **National Agro-Biosecurity Authority (NABA)** for regulatory oversight and compliance.
3. Develop and deploy an **Annual Agrosecurity Resilience Index**, tracking preparedness and response across states.
4. Allocate targeted **funding for infrastructure, R&D**, and emergency response.

5. Launch **innovation grants** for diagnostic tools, pathogen sensors, drone surveillance systems, and cold-chain monitoring technologies.

8.2 Integrated Bio-Surveillance Infrastructure

Effective agility in agro-biosecurity depends on multilayer surveillance platforms combining field tools, labs, and modeling.

8.2.1 Four-Tiered Infrastructure

Table 3:

Tier	*Institutional Node*	*Functions*	*Lead Agencies*
1	District-level KVKs & veterinary posts	Field testing (LAMP/RT-PCR), data entry	KVKs, State Agri. Depts
2	Regional biosecurity labs (ICAR, NPPO)	Genomic sequencing, pathogen characterization	ICAR Institutes, NPPO
3	NASM Data & Alert Center	Data collation, GIS dashboards, threat alerts	NASM, NDMA, ICAR
4	Predictive Analytics Unit	Risk modeling using climate, crop, trade data	ICAR–IASRI, DRDO

- **Tier 1:** Equip 700+ KVKs with rapid kits, supported by apps linked to District Control Rooms.
- **Tier 2:** Up-skill State Reference Labs with genomic capacities; align with NPPO protocols.
- **Tier 3:** Establish a national platform for trend analysis and alerts.
- **Tier 4:** Use NDMA and ICAR's modeling units to simulate outbreak scenarios and optimize responses (Gupta & Sankaran, 2021).

8.2.2 Digital Integration and Sensor Networks

- Deploy **IoT-based micro-devices** in farms and cold storage for environmental monitoring.
- Integrate **National Pest Surveillance System (NPSS)** launched in 2024 with **NASM** for automated pest-risk tracking via AI/ML (Press Information Bureau, 2024).

8.3 Community-Based Agro-Bio Intelligence

Empowering locals transforms passive farmers into active threat detectors.

8.3.1 Agro-Bio Warriors

- Recruit trained community members across 600,000 villages.
- Train them using protocols derived from **NDMA's Biological Disaster Guidelines**, supplemented with guided kits for QR-coded sample collection **(NDMA, 2008).**

8.3.2 Farmer-Centric Reporting Tools

- Maintain a **geo-tagging app** for smartphone submissions, alerting labs when samples are flagged.
- Expand upon **Kisan Call Centre (KCC)** telephonic data, which already hosts over 61% of farmers, to include text and image uploads (Adhikari et al., 2021).

8.3.3 Incentive Systems

- Issue **certificates and subsidized inputs** to verified reporters.
- A **"community credit score"** reflects district-level engagement, increasing priority funding were utilized most.

8.4 Risk Communication and Public Awareness

Transparent and proactive communication fortifies defences.

8.4.1 Multi-Channel Communications

- **AgroAlert Radio Broadcasts:** Local-language bulletins extending surveillance reach.
- **SMS & WhatsApp Updates:** Short advisories based on lab-confirmed cases.
- **BDAT Posters:** Strategically placed visuals at grain markets, dairies, depots, and panchayat offices.
- **Village Drills:** Town hall tabletop simulations testing community response capabilities.

These were tested in human viral outbreaks in accordance with NDMA's guidelines, and the alerts caused a 45% increase in awareness (NDMA, 2008).

8.4.2 Media & Social Platforms

- Coordinate with **Doordarshan** and **All India Radio** for high visibility.
- Launch a dedicated **NASM Telegram/WhatsApp channel** for real-time alerts and updates.

8.5 Academic Curriculum Integration

The development of talent is essential for long-term resilience.

- **BSc Agriculture & Extension programs** adopt core courses on agroterrorism: pre-harvest detection, legal frameworks, and response logistics.
- **Diploma Courses** for plant protection/veterinary disciplines include lab diagnostics and risk modeling techniques.
- **Postgraduate Research:** Fund master's and doctoral work on genetic surveillance, predictive modeling, and agro-forensic systems.
- **Professional Fellowship Programs** under NASM supporting overseas training and specialization.

8.6 Monitoring & Evaluation (M&E)

Key Performance Indicators (KPIs) guide adaptive improvements.

- **Detection Speed** – % cases lab-confirmed within 7 days.
- **Lab Coverage** – % districts with operational diagnostic facilities.
- **Community Engagement** – number of validated alerts received.
- **Education Penetration** – number of institutions with curriculum integration.
- **Resilience Index** – national and state performance scores.

Annual performance audits, published by NASM and submitted to the agriculture and home affairs committees, will ensure accountability.

8.7 International Alignment and Collaboration\

Safeguarding food systems requires global cooperation.

- **OIE Reporting:** Ensure timely livestock disease notifications.
- **IPPC Quarantine Standards:** Enhance phytosanitary clearance protocols for imports/exports.
- **BWC Convention Compliance:** Transparent declarations on biocontainment labs such as DRDO's BSL-4 facility in Gwalior (Times of India, 2024).
- Regional partnerships via **SAARC/BIMSTEC** to share pathogen intelligence and co-manage outbreaks.

India is positioned to lead **FAO/WHO** advisory councils due to its expanding bioeconomy (Times of India, 2024).

8.8 Funding Mechanisms and Incentives

Sustainability demands smart financing.

- Reroute **PMFBY digital infrastructure** funds to support Tier 1–2 deployment.

- Use **G20 climate/social resilience funds** to fund priority interventions in agro biosecurity.
- Provide **tax incentives and grants** to startups developing diagnostics, AI tools, and response devices.
- Establish a **Revolving R&D Fund** within NASM for short-cycle innovation funding.

8.9 Implementation Phases

Table 4:

Phase	Timeline	Activities
Pilot	Year 1	Launch in Punjab, Maharashtra, West Bengal, Telangana, Odisha; test Tier-1 diagnostics, apps, drills.
Scale Up	Years 2–3	Expand labs and surveillance systems nationwide; integrate digital platforms; launch National Agrosecurity Index.
Institutional Embedment	Years 4–5	Curriculum rollout; model integration; legal frameworks; multi-state drills.
Consolidation	Year 6+	Annual audit; continuous improvement; international policy engagement.

8.10 Addressing Risks and Challenges

Risk 1: Agency Fragmentation

Solution: Legalize NASM through Parliamentary Act; formalize coordination via mandatory performance metrics.

Risk 2: Inadequate Capacity

Solution: Launch training programs, hire specialized staff, and equip labs with national standards.

Risk 3: Data & Privacy Concerns

Solution: Implement end-to-end encryption, anonymized reporting, and data-sharing MOUs with affected stakeholders.

Risk 4: Sustained Financing

Solution: Ring-fence budget lines in crop and livestock insurance portfolios, with NASM oversight.

Conclusion

Agroterrorism resilience demands systematic alignment—from central governance and cutting-edge technology to community participation and global standards. Implementing NASM, the layered surveillance system, education integration, and cooperative frameworks positions India to effectively anticipate and neutralize agro-biothreats. This policy blueprint prioritizes food

security, farmer welfare, and public health—ensuring agrarian stability in the face of emerging biological threats.

Chapter 9: Legal Framework and Agroterrorism Law in India

Dibyendu Nayak[1*] and Sounak Chakraborty[2]

[1*] School of Agriculture, Lovely Professional University, Phagwara, Punjab-144001, India

[2]School of Agriculture, Lovely Professional University, Phagwara, Punjab-144001, India

***Corresponding author**: dibyendunayak05@gmail.com

Agroterrorism—the deliberate biological sabotage of agricultural systems—remains a legal blindspot in India. Current legislation, including the Indian Penal Code (IPC) and Unlawful Activities (Prevention) Act (UAPA), lacks explicit provisions to address such threats. Similarly, existing phytosanitary and veterinary import regulations focus on accidental biohazard prevention rather than intentional attack. This chapter examines relevant laws, analyzes these gaps, suggests a specific Agro–Bio Threat Act (ABTA), and takes ideas from global models like the U.S. Agroterrorism Preparedness Act.

9.1 Gaps in the Indian Penal Code (IPC) and Unlawful Activities (Prevention) Act (UAPA) Regarding Agroterrorism\

India's legal system for handling national threats is mainly regulated by the **Unlawful Activities (Prevention) Act (UAPA), 1967**, and the **Indian Penal Code (IPC), 1860**. These frameworks were primarily developed to address traditional criminal offenses and terrorist threats that target

human casualties, state instability, and political insurgency. However, as India's agricultural sector becomes increasingly vulnerable to biological, chemical, and ecological sabotage, a concerning legislative gap appears. The current provisions of the IPC and UAPA do not specifically recognize agroterrorism—the deliberate use of biological agents or ecological disruption to destroy crops, livestock, or rural economies—as a distinct or punishable offense.

9.1.1. The IPC and Its Limitations on Agroterrorism

The IPC, the foundation of Indian criminal law, provides a comprehensive framework for the prosecution of environmental damage, criminal negligence, and sabotage. However, agroterrorism does not appropriately fall into any one category. For example:

- **Section 268** (Public nuisance) and **Section 269/270** (Negligent or malignant acts likely to spread infection of disease) may apply to accidental biohazards but not intentional agroterrorism acts.
- **Section 425** (Mischief) and **Section 427** (Mischief causing damage over ₹50) may be invoked for damage to property (e.g., crops or cattle), but fail to capture the scale, intent, or biosecurity risk inherent in agroterrorism (Singh & Gupta, 2022).

- **Environmental sabotage**, while damaging, would likely fall under the **Environment Protection Act (EPA), 1986**, but not IPC directly.

Critically, IPC lacks terminology and clauses specific to **biological warfare against agriculture**, nor does it mention **agricultural biohazards**, leaving authorities ill-equipped to legally define or prosecute such threats under this code.

9.1.2. UAPA and Its Inapplicability to Agricultural Sabotage

The **UAPA** is India's primary anti-terror law and is designed to address threats against the sovereignty and integrity of India. The law defines **terrorist acts** in **Section 15**, which includes actions intended to threaten the **unity**, **integrity**, **security**, or **sovereignty of India**, or to **strike terror among people.**

While these definitions are broad, they focus almost entirely on:

- **Explosives, firearms, and weapons.**
- **Political, ethnic, or religious motivations.**
- Acts that result in **loss of human life or damage to government infrastructure.**

Agroterrorism may not directly cause immediate loss of human life but can result in:

- **Collapse of regional economies.**
- **Food insecurity and inflation.**
- **Long-term environmental and ecological harm.**
- **Psychological and financial distress in rural populations.**

Unfortunately, authorities cannot use **UAPA** as a legal framework to charge people who commit acts of agroterrorism unless those acts have a direct connection to larger terror networks because it does not contain terms like **"bio-agent", "crop sabotage"," livestock biothreats"**, or **"agricultural terrorism".**

9.1.3. Recent Incidents and the Legal Vacuum

Several recent incidents, such as the **intentional introduction of Fall Armyworm in maize belts** (Suby et al., 2020) or smuggling of **non-native pathogens in horticultural imports**, suggest **biological sabotage**, but enforcement agencies lack clarity on **how to classify, investigate, and prosecute** these threats under either IPC or UAPA.

Moreover, the lack of forensic biosecurity components within law enforcement makes it more **difficult to gather and attribute evidence** that is required for prosecution of terrorism-related charges. At the moment, organizations such as the **National Investigation Agency (NIA)** lack the authority to look into **agro-biological threats** unless there is a **connection to human casualties.**

9.1.4. The Global Contrast

Countries like the **United States** have more specific laws, such as the **Public Health Security and Bioterrorism Preparedness and Response Act (2002)** and sections under the **Homeland Security Act**, which define agroterrorism and prescribe punishments for the introduction of pathogens to crops and livestock (Monke, 2005). India's failure to incorporate such provisions creates a **legislative asymmetry** in an age of increasing agro-biological threats.

Comparative Overview of Legal Provisions (India vs. USA)

Table 5: Comparative Overview of Legal Provisions (India vs. USA)

Criteria	*Indian IPC & UAPA*	*U.S. Agroterrorism Laws*
Explicit mention of agroterrorism	❌ Not mentioned	✅ Clearly defined under Bioterrorism Act (2002)
Coverage of crop/livestock threats	❌ Indirect under "mischief"/environment laws	✅ Covered as national security threat
Legal investigative authority	❌ Unclear for agri-biothreats	✅ FBI, USDA, Homeland Security involved
Forensic biosecurity protocols	❌ Absent	✅ Established agro-bio forensics protocols
Agro-bio terrorism penalties	❌ Undefined	✅ Severe penalties under federal law

9.1.5. Need for a Specific Legal Definition and Framework

To bridge this legal vacuum, the following are proposed:

- Definition of **agroterrorism** as a standalone offense under IPC or a new **Agro-Bio Threat Act.**
- Empowering agencies like the **NIA**, **IB**, and **others related to agricultural biosecurity** to act as investigative bodies.
- Integration of **Krishi Vigyan Kendras (KVKs)** and **ICAR institutions** into legal frameworks as advisory and expert entities.
- Mandatory reporting mechanisms through **district collectors and panchayats** in suspected cases of agro-biological sabotage.

9.2 Review: Plant Quarantine Order (2003) and Livestock Import Regulations

9.2.1 Plant Quarantine (Regulation of Import into India) Order, 2003

This Order, under the **Destructive Insects and Pests Act (1914),** modernized India's plant import controls to align with the **IPPC** and **WTO-SPS** standards**:**

- Requires **Pest Risk Analysis (PRA)** for seeds, germplasm, GMOs, live insects, and plant material (FAOLEX, 2003).
- Defines schedules for prohibited, restricted, and conditional imports (e.g., 590 pests, 61 weed species in the 2003 Order).
- Extends **post-entry quarantine** to treat or destroy contaminated stock.

However, its focus remains on **unintentional biohazards**, lacking legal provisions for **intentional release or tampering of imported materials**. The Directorate of Plant Protection is reportedly weakly staffed, especially at land and sea entry points, complicating implementation**.**

9.2.2 Livestock Import Regulations

The **Animal Quarantine & Certification Service (AQCS)**, under the Department of Animal Husbandry and Dairying, focuses on preventing zoonotic disease entry through imports:

- Certifies animals and animal-origin products.
- Applies quarantine measures at borders.
- Lacks capacity for **forensic pathogen investigation** tied to agri-biothreats or terrorism.

Thus, while limiting cross-border disease risks, AQCS does not account for deliberate sabotage via biological agents**.**

9.3 Proposal: Agro–Bio Threat Act (ABTA) – A National Legal Framework to Recognize Agroterrorism as a Form of Terrorist Attack

9.3.1. Introduction

Agroterrorism—defined as the intentional introduction of pests, pathogens, or contaminants into the agricultural ecosystem to cause large-scale disruption—remains a blind spot in India's legislative security framework. Neither the **Indian Penal Code (IPC)** or newly introduced **Bharatiya Nyaya Sanhita (BNS)** nor the **Unlawful Activities (Prevention) Act (UAPA)** currently addresses deliberate acts of biological sabotage in agriculture as terrorist acts. In response to this legal vacuum, this chapter proposes the creation of a new national legal instrument titled the **Agro–Bio Threat Act (ABTA)**, modeled on the structure and severity of the UAPA, with specific recognition of biological, ecological, and agricultural sabotage as acts of terrorism**.**

9.3.2. The Rationale Behind ABTA

- **Economic Relevance:** Agriculture employs over 45% of India's population (Ministry of Agriculture & Farmers Welfare, 2023). A targeted biological attack can cripple regional economies, inflate food prices, and create panic.
- **Biosecurity Vulnerability:** India's porous borders, seed import dependencies, and limited bio-surveillance infrastructure make it vulnerable to agro-biothreats.
- **International Standards:** Countries like the U.S. recognize agroterrorism under acts like the **Public Health Security and Bioterrorism Preparedness and Response Act (2002)**, and India must adopt a comparable framework (Monke, 2005).

9.3.3. Proposed Legal Framework: The Agro–Bio Threat Act (ABTA)

The **Agro–Bio Threat Act (ABTA)** will be a special law passed by the Indian Parliament to provide a comprehensive legal and operational framework for prevention, detection, investigation, and prosecution of agro-biological threats and agroterrorism.

Section A: Definitions

1) Agroterrorism: Any deliberate act intended to **destroy**, **damage**, **contaminate**, or **disrupt crops**, **livestock**, **fisheries**, **soil health**, or **agricultural inputs** using **biological**, **chemical**, **radiological**, or **ecological** agents with the intent to:

- **Cause economic loss.**
- **Install fear among farming communities.**
- **Destabilize food security or trade systems.**
- **Undermine public confidence in agricultural resilience.**

2) Biological Agent: Any microorganism, virus, fungus, toxin, genetically modified organism, pest or any foreign species of plant or animal used for the purpose of agricultural sabotage.

3) Agro–Bio Threat Organization: Any individual or group that plans or carries out agro-biological sabotage or supports such acts.

Section B: Punishable Offenses under ABTA

Table 6:

Offense	Proposed Punishment
Intentional release of pests/pathogens to disrupt crops/livestock	Imprisonment for life + ₹25 lakh fine
Use of foreign-origin GMOs/toxins without license for sabotage	Minimum 10 years RI extendable to life
Deliberate poisoning of agri-inputs (e.g., fertilizers, irrigation water)	Minimum 20 years RI

Coordinating with foreign agencies for agro-biothreats	Life imprisonment + property attachment
Harboring, financing, or training agroterror suspects	10 years RI + ₹10 lakh fine
Dissemination of threat materials (manuals, bio-lab access)	7–15 years RI
False alarms or hoaxes related to agroterrorism	3 years RI + ₹1 lakh fine

Note: *RI = Rigorous Imprisonment*

Section C: Designated Investigating and Adjudicating Authorities

1) **National Agrosecurity Task Force (NASTF)** to be created under Ministry of Home Affairs in collaboration with Ministry of Agriculture.

2) NASTF will include ICAR scientists, NIA officers, and agricultural biosecurity experts.

3) **Special Agroterrorism Courts (SACs)** to be established in affected states for fast-track trials.

4) Provisions for **preventive detention**, **surveillance**, and **property attachment**, like UAPA.

Section D: Whistleblower and Witness Protection

- Any **agronomist, farmer,** or **field-level officer** reporting agroterrorist activity will be granted anonymity and immunity.
- Dedicated **witness protection fund** to assist field informants and whistleblowers.

Section E: Integration with Existing Laws

- ABTA will override overlapping clauses of IPC, UAPA, and Plant Quarantine Order (2003) where necessary.
- ABTA will mandate cooperation with:
    - **DRDO** (bio-defense support),
    - **FSSAI** (food chain monitoring),
    - **Customs Department** (border control for illegal agro-bio imports).

9.3.4. Proposed Organizational Model under ABTA

Ministry of Home Affairs
↓
National Agrosecurity Task Force (NASTF)
↓
Zonal Agroterrorism Control Units (ZACUs) at state level
↓
District Agrosecurity Cells (with KVKs, Panchayats)

9.3.5. International Benchmarks: Learning from the U.S. Public Health Security and Bioterrorism Preparedness and Response Act (2002)

The **U.S. Public Health Security and Bioterrorism Preparedness and Response Act (2002)** empowered the **Department of Homeland Security**, in coordination with the **USDA**, to create a surveillance and response mechanism specifically for agricultural bioterror threats. It includes:

- The National Veterinary Stockpile.
- National Plant Diagnostic Network.
- Agro-bioterror threat scenario simulations and drills.

India can **replicate and localize** these components under **ABTA** using existing institutions like **ICAR**, **KVKs**, and **Agricultural Universities.**

9.4 International Case Studies: U.S. Agroterrorism Legislation

The **United States** is one of the few nations to systematically recognize and prepare for **agroterrorism as a national security threat**. Following the September 11 attacks in 2001 and the subsequent anthrax incidents, U.S. policymakers broadened the definition of terrorism to include threats against the food and agriculture sector. This section examines the evolution of U.S. agroterrorism-related legislation and policy frameworks, providing key insights for the development of similar structures in India, including the proposed **Agro–Bio Threat Act (ABTA).**

9.4.1. Homeland Security Presidential Directive 9 (HSPD-9)

In **2004**, the **U.S. government** issued **Homeland Security Presidential Directive 9**, which formally recognized agriculture and food as **critical infrastructure. HSPD-9** directed multiple federal agencies—including the **Department of Homeland Security (DHS)**, **Department of Agriculture (USDA)**, and **Department of Health and Human Services (HHS)**—to:

- Develop **surveillance and early-warning systems** for plant and animal diseases.
- Build a **National Veterinary Stockpile (NVS)** for animal emergency preparedness.
- Conduct **vulnerability assessments** for food systems.
- Promote **recovery systems** for agricultural production (White House, 2004).

This directive institutionalized agroterrorism preparedness as a cross-sectoral, multi-agency national priority.

9.4.2. Public Health Security and Bioterrorism Preparedness and Response Act (2002)

Also known as the **Bioterrorism Act**, this law was enacted in the wake of anthrax attacks and aimed to bolster national readiness against biological threats, including those impacting agriculture. Key provisions relevant to agroterrorism include:

- Establishment of a **"select agent"** list, which includes biological agents harmful to plants and animals.

- Regulation and registration of all entities possessing or transferring select agents.
- **Mandatory background checks** for individuals working in labs handling select agents.
- Increased funding for agricultural biosecurity research.

This act laid the legal foundation for secure handling and transport of high-risk agricultural pathogens.

9.4.3. Agroterrorism Prevention Acts of 2001 & 2005 (Unenacted Bills)

Although not passed into law, these legislative proposals were designed to directly criminalize acts of agroterrorism. The proposed bills sought to:

- Create a **federal definition of agroterrorism**.
- Enhance penalties for crimes involving deliberate harm to crops, livestock, or agricultural infrastructure.
- Establish a **National Agroterrorism Response Center** under USDA.

These bills were influential in shaping subsequent executive orders and research priorities.

9.4.4. National Plant Diagnostic Network (NPDN)

The **National Plant Diagnostic Network**, established under **USDA** and **Land-Grant Universities**, is a critical surveillance tool for early detection of biothreats. It includes:

- A real-time, nationwide lab network for **plant disease diagnosis.**
- Training for first responders and extension personnel.
- A central database to report unusual pathogen activity.

NPDN plays a frontline role in identifying, verifying, and responding to suspicious outbreaks in crops.

9.4.5. Project BioShield Act (2004) and PAHPRA (2013)

These acts primarily focus on medical countermeasures, but include provisions for funding agricultural bioterror countermeasures, especially for zoonotic threats and foodborne pathogens. Key features:

- **$5.6 billion** authorized to support **research and procurement of countermeasures.**
- Encouraged private sector development of vaccines and diagnostics.
- Provided **liability protections** for manufacturers of agricultural defense tools.

9.4.6. USDA Agrosecurity Programs

The **USDA's Animal and Plant Health Inspection Service (APHIS)** leads federal efforts on plant and animal biosecurity. Programs include:

- The **Select Agent Program** (in collaboration with CDC).
- **APHIS' Smuggling Interdiction and Trade Compliance (SITC)** program to intercept illegal agri-imports.
- Support for **agroterrorism scenario training exercises and bioforensics laboratories.**

9.4.7. U.S Vs India

Table 7 :

Aspect	U.S. System	India (Current)	Recommendation via ABTA
Legal recognition of agroterrorism	☑ Bioterrorism Act & HSPD-9	✕ None	Enact Agro–Bio Threat Act (ABTA)
Surveillance network	☑ NPDN, APHIS, DHS	✕ Fragmented (ICAR, KVKs)	Create unified bio-surveillance grid
Select agent regulation	☑ CDC-USDA dual authority	✕ No such classification	Develop licensed bio-agent registry
Forensic and response capacity	☑ USDA/NVS & DHS rapid teams	✕ DRDO limited to military pathogens	Create agro-bio forensics task force
Scenario-based drills and training	☑ Regular USDA and DHS simulations	✕ Not formalized	Annual national simulation exercises

Conclusion: Securing Agriculture Against Emerging Threats

Agriculture has historically been a symbol of sustenance and civilization. In the modern era, it has also emerged as a potential target in the evolving threat of unconventional warfare. This book has comprehensively mapped the rising threat of **agroterrorism**—defined as the deliberate use of biological, chemical, or technological means to attack agricultural systems—and demonstrated why it must be integrated into **India's national security and public policy discourse.**

Chapter Summaries and Synthesis

In **Chapter 1**, we established the foundational understanding of agroterrorism, differentiating it from bioterrorism by its direct targeting of **agricultural assets** rather than human populations. By aligning with global definitions from **FAO**, **WHO**, **UNODC**, and **USDA**, the chapter framed agroterrorism as a specialized domain of non-conventional warfare, demanding unique prevention and response mechanisms.

Chapter 2 documented historical precedents, including the **1984 Oregon Salmonella outbreak** and the **UK Foot-and-Mouth Disease outbreak of 2001**, underscoring how subtle biological agents can be weaponized to destabilize societies. Case typologies—crops, livestock, ecosystems—demonstrated that agroterrorism can take many forms, each with unique risks and ripple effects.

In **Chapter 3**, we explored the **multiple threat vectors**—biological agents, chemical toxins, and cyber-attack mechanisms. From fungal pathogens like Puccinia graminis to IoT-based smart farming sabotage, this chapter highlighted the expanding frontlines of agricultural warfare, showing that bio-threats now transcend microbes and enter the digital realm.

Chapter 4 localized the threat to India by assessing its agricultural vulnerability. Using real ICAR data, we proposed the **National Bio-Economic Fragility Index (NBEFI)**—a composite metric to assess regional vulnerabilities based on **agro-economic dependence**, **biosecurity gaps**, and **infrastructure bottlenecks**. India's seed chains, mandis, and livestock zones remain critically exposed to targeted sabotage.

Chapter 5 delved into the **socioeconomic implications**, revealing how agroterrorism could trigger inflation, distress migration, farmer suicides, and regional hunger crises. It also evaluated institutional stress points in **NFSA** and **PDS** and revealed how a single agricultural shock could ripple into nutrition, trade, and ecosystem services.

Chapter 6 examined **international legal instruments**, such as the **Biological Weapons Convention (BWC)** and the **International Plant Protection Convention (IPPC)**, suggesting how India can model its agro-biosecurity frameworks after successful examples. **Early Detection and Rapid Response Systems (EDRRs)** and **phytosanitary technologies** were discussed as first lines of defense.

Chapter 7 addressed India's institutional architecture, noting the partial readiness of organizations like **NDMA, ICAR, FSSAI**, and **DRDO**. While valuable frameworks like the Plant Quarantine Order (2003) exist, India lacks a unified agrosecurity mission and suffers from inconsistent contingency protocols and bio-intelligence deployment at the grassroots.

In **Chapter 8**, we laid out a detailed strategic roadmap, proposing the **National Agrosecurity Mission (NASM)** and recommending major reforms: bio-surveillance networks, farmer-facing risk communication platforms, and curriculum inclusion in agricultural education. Interdisciplinary action between scientists, policymakers, and farming communities was emphasized as central to resilience.

Chapter 9 identified severe **legal voids** in India's penal system. Neither the IPC nor UAPA currently classify agroterrorism as terrorism. As a remedy, the proposed **Agro–Bio Threat Act (ABTA)** was detailed, outlining punishable offenses, investigative mechanisms, and parallels with U.S. frameworks like the **Homeland Security Presidential Directive 9 (HSPD-9)**. A comparative analysis with U.S. and global systems revealed India's legislative lag and the urgent need for tailored lawmaking.

The Need for Integration: Agriculture as National Security

Agriculture is no longer merely an economic sector—it is a **strategic national asset**. With climate variability, global trade disruptions, and transboundary pest/pathogen movement increasing, India's food systems face growing risks. Agroterrorism is a slow, silent disruptor with the potential to:

- Destroy trust in food safety.
- Collapse rural economies.
- Incite civil unrest due to food shortages.
- Harm international export reputations.

This book has argued for the **full integration of agrosecurity into the national security apparatus**, demanding coordination between the Ministries of Home Affairs, Agriculture, Environment, Science & Technology, and Defence.

Final Recommendations: Building a Biosecure Bharat

To safeguard India's agricultural backbone and rural resilience, we recommend:

1) **Immediate enactment of the Agro–Bio Threat Act (ABTA)** to criminalize agroterrorism with defined provisions and national enforcement.

2) **Creation of the National Agrosecurity Mission (NASM)** for centralized planning, training, and response.

3) **Biointelligence training for field officers, farmers, and panchayats,** including digital risk-reporting tools and incentives.

4) Academic inclusion: Agrosecurity modules in BSc Agriculture, Extension Education, and Agricultural Engineering.

5) International collaboration with FAO, USDA, and INTERPOL on transboundary agro-biosecurity protocols and drills.

Agroterrorism is not merely a theoretical threat—it is a real, emerging domain of sabotage that targets the lifeblood of our civilization: food. Recognizing, preparing for, and legislating against agroterrorism is not an option—it is a necessity. India must now move from vulnerability to vigilance, from reaction to prevention, and from fragmentation to institutional cohesion.

This book is a call to action—to scientists, lawmakers, farmers, and citizens—to build a resilient, bio-secure agricultural future for generations to come.

Jai Kisan. Jai Vigyan. Jai Suraksha.

References

Chapter 1: Conceptual Framework of Agroterrorism

1) Chalk, P. (2004). Agroterrorism: What is the Threat and What Can Be Done About It? RAND Corporation.

2) FAO & WHO. (2010). Framework for the Development and Implementation of National Food Safety Emergency Response Plans. Rome: Food and Agriculture Organization of the United Nations.

3) Kesan, J. P., & Hayes, C. M. (2012). Mitigative Counterstriking: Self-Defense and Deterrence in Cyberspace. Harvard Journal of Law & Technology, 25(2), 429–475.

4) Monke, J. (2005). Agroterrorism: Threats and Preparedness. Congressional Research Service Report for Congress.

5) MoAFW. (2023). Annual Report 2022-23. Ministry of Agriculture and Farmers Welfare, Government of India.

6) UNODA. (2017). Biological Weapons Convention: Confidence-Building Measures. United Nations Office for Disarmament Affairs.

7) UNODC. (2020). Emerging Threats and Transnational Crimes: Food Chain Sabotage in Conflict Zones. Vienna: United Nations Office on Drugs and Crime.

8) USDA. (2018). USDA Agroterrorism Preparedness and Response. U.S. Department of Agriculture, Washington, D.C.

9) Wheelis M. (2002). Biological warfare at the 1346 siege of Caffa. Emerging infectious diseases, 8(9), 971–975. https://doi.org/10.3201/eid0809.010536

Chapter 2: Documented Incidents and Historical Precedents

1) FAO. (2010). Cassava diseases in East Africa: Emerging threats and mitigation. Food and Agriculture Organization of the United Nations.

2) FAO & WHO. (2016). Framework for developing national food safety emergency response plans. Rome: FAO.

3) FAO. (2020). African Swine Fever in China: Impact and response. FAO EMPRES Report

4) Singh RP, Hodson DP, Huerta-Espino J, Jin Y, Bhavani S, Njau P, Herrera-Foessel S, Singh PK, Singh S, Govindan V. The emergence of Ug99 races of the stem rust fungus is a threat to

world wheat production. Annu Rev Phytopathol. 2011; 49:465-81. doi: 10.1146/annurev-phyto-072910-095423. PMID: 21568701.

5) Thompson D, Muriel P, Russell D, Osborne P, Bromley A, Rowland M, Creigh-Tyte S, Brown C. Economic costs of the foot and mouth disease outbreak in the United Kingdom in 2001. Rev Sci Tech. 2002 Dec;21(3):675-87. doi: 10.20506/rst.21.3.1353. PMID: 12523706.

6) Wheelis M. (2002). Biological warfare at the 1346 siege of Caffa. Emerging infectious diseases, 8(9), 971–975. https://doi.org/10.3201/eid0809.010536

7) Török, T. J., Tauxe, R. V., Wise, R. P., Livengood, J. R., Sokolow, R., Mauvais, S., Birkness, K. A., Skeels, M. R., Horan, J. M., & Foster, L. R. (1997). A large community outbreak of salmonellosis caused by intentional contamination of restaurant salad bars. JAMA, 278(5), 389–395. https://doi.org/10.1001/jama.1997.03550050051033

Chapter 3: Threat Vectors and Mechanisms of Attack

1) Gebreyes, W. A., Jackwood, D., de Oliveira, C. J. B., Lee, C. W., Hoet, A. E., & Thakur, S. (2020). Molecular epidemiology of infectious zoonotic and livestock diseases. Microbiology Spectrum, 8(2), 10-1128.

2) de Jong, J. C., McCormack, B. J., Smirnoff, N., & Talbot, N. J. (1997). Glycerol generates turgor in rice blast. Nature, 389(6648), 244-244.

3) Melotto, M., Zhang, L., Oblessuc, P. R., & He, S. Y. (2017). Stomatal defense a decade later. Plant physiology, 174(2), 561-571.

4) Chen, C. Y., Liu, Y. Q., Song, W. M., Chen, D. Y., Chen, F. Y., Chen, X. Y., ... & Mao, Y. B. (2019). An effector from cotton bollworm oral secretion impairs host plant defense signaling. Proceedings of the National Academy of Sciences, 116(28), 14331-14338.

5) Whitfield, A. E., Falk, B. W., & Rotenberg, D. (2015). Insect vector-mediated transmission of plant viruses. Virology, 479, 278-289.

6) Bharatbhai, P. P. (2019). Investigation on Seed Borne Nature of Pepper mild mottle virus and Assessment of Yield Losses in Capsicum (Doctoral dissertation, Chaudhary Sarwan Kumar Himachal Pradesh Krishi Vishvavidyalaya).

7) Derevnina, L., Contreras, M. P., Adachi, H., Upson, J., Cruces, A. V., Xie, R., ... & Kamoun, S. (2021). Plant pathogens convergently evolved to counteract redundant nodes of an NLR immune receptor network. PLoS biology, 19(8), e3001136.

8) Snelders, N. C., Rovenich, H., & Thomma, B. P. (2022). Microbiota manipulation through the secretion of effector proteins is fundamental to the wealth of lifestyles in the fungal kingdom. FEMS microbiology reviews, 46(5), fuac022.

9) Chanclud, E., & Morel, J. B. (2016). Plant hormones: a fungal point of view. Molecular Plant Pathology, 17(8), 1289-1297.

10) Singh, S. P., & Singh, M. K. (2020). Soil pollution and human health. Plant responses to soil pollution, 205-220.

11) Chaudhary, P., Xu, M., Ahamad, L., Chaudhary, A., Kumar, G., Adeleke, B. S., ... & Abou Fayssal, S. (2023). Application of synthetic consortia for improvement of soil fertility, pollution remediation, and agricultural productivity: a review. Agronomy, 13(3), 643.

12) Sarkar, B., Mukhopadhyay, R., Ramanayaka, S., Bolan, N., & Ok, Y. S. (2021). The role of soils in the disposition, sequestration and decontamination of environmental contaminants. Philosophical Transactions of the Royal Society B, 376(1834), 20200177.

13) Miller, H., Dias, K., Hare, H., Borton, M. A., Blotevogel, J., Danforth, C., ... & Borch, T. (2020). Reusing oil and gas produced water for agricultural irrigation: Effects on soil health and the soil microbiome. Science of the Total Environment, 722, 137888.

14) Ojo, A., Nnamso-Ubokudom, M., & Nzekwe, O. (2024). Geochemical assessments and human health risk evaluations of selected farm soils within the Abuja metropolis, North- central, Nigeria. African Scientific Reports, 232-232.

15) Anjaria, P., & Vaghela, S. (2024). Toxicity of agrochemicals: Impact on environment and human health. Journal of Toxicological Studies, 2(1), 250-250.

16) Alahmadi, A. N., Rehman, S. U., Alhazmi, H. S., Glynn, D. G., Shoaib, H., & Solé, P. (2022). Cyber-security threats and side-channel attacks for digital agriculture. Sensors, 22(9), 3520.

17) Gupta, M., Abdelsalam, M., Khorsandroo, S., & Mittal, S. (2020). Security and privacy in smart farming: Challenges and opportunities. IEEE access, 8, 34564-34584.

18) Rudrakar, S., & Rughani, P. (2023). IoT based agriculture (Ag-IoT): A detailed study on architecture, security and forensics. Information Processing in Agriculture.

19) Sontowski, S., Gupta, M., Chukkapalli, S. S. L., Abdelsalam, M., Mittal, S., Joshi, A., & Sandhu, R. (2020, December). Cyber-attacks on smart farming infrastructure. In 2020 IEEE 6th International Conference on Collaboration and Internet Computing (CIC) (pp. 135-143). IEEE.

20) Aldhyani, T. H., & Alkahtani, H. (2023). Cyber security for detecting distributed denial of service attacks in agriculture 4.0: Deep learning model. Mathematics, 11(1), 233.

21) Scheffer, R. P., & Livingston, R. S. (1984). Host-selective toxins and their role in plant diseases. Science, 223(4631), 17-21.

22) Mitchell, R. E. (1984). The relevance of non-host-specific toxins in the expression of virulence by pathogens. Annual Review of Phytopathology, 22(1), 215-245.

Chapter 4: Agricultural Vulnerability Assessment: Indian Context

1) Kumar, N., Chander, Y., Kumar, R., Khandelwal, N., Riyesh, T., Chaudhary, K., ... & Tripathi, B. N. (2021). Isolation and characterization of lumpy skin disease virus from cattle in India. PloS one, 16(1), e0241022.

2) Memish, Z. A., Kattan, R. F., Ebrahim, S. H., Sharma, A., Azhar, E. I., & Zumla, A. (2024). Proactive surveillance for avian influenza H5N1 and other priority pathogens at mass gathering events. The Lancet Public Health, 9(6), e350-e352.

3) Varadan, R. J., & Kumar, P. (2015). Mapping agricultural vulnerability of Tamil Nadu, India to climate change: a dynamic approach to take forward the vulnerability assessment methodology. Climatic change, 129, 159-181.

4) Cheng, W., Li, Y., Zuo, W., Du, G., & Stanny, M. (2024). Spatio-temporal detection of agricultural disaster vulnerability in the world and implications for developing climate- resilient agriculture. Science of the Total Environment, 928, 172412.

5) Kumar, A., Kumar, A., Mann, K., & Mohanasundari, T. (2024). Analysing district-level climate vulnerability pattern in Madhya Pradesh, India, based on agricultural and socio-economic indicators. Environmental Monitoring and Assessment, 196(6), 528.

6) Senapati, U., & Das, T. K. (2024). Geospatial assessment of agricultural drought vulnerability using integrated three-dimensional model in the upper Dwarakeshwar river basin in West Bengal, India. Environmental Science and Pollution Research, 31(41), 54061-54088.

Chapter 5: Socioeconomic and Food Security Implications of Agroterrorism

1) FAO. (2021). The State of Food Security and Nutrition in the World 2021. Rome: FAO.

2) MoAFW. (2022). Annual Report 2021–22. Ministry of Agriculture & Farmers Welfare, Government of India.

3) NCRB. (2023). Accidental Deaths and Suicides in India – 2022. National Crime Records Bureau, Ministry of Home Affairs.

4) NFHS-5. (2021). National Family Health Survey (2019-21). Ministry of Health & Family Welfare.

5) Reserve Bank of India. (2023). Handbook of Statistics on Indian Economy: CPI Components.

6) WHO. (2019). Global Nutrition Policy Review. World Health Organization.

Chapter 6: Risk Management and International Frameworks

1) FAO. (2023). International Plant Protection Convention. Rome: FAO.

2) Trump, B. D., Galaitsi, S. E., Appleton, E., Bleijs, D. A., Florin, M. V., Gollihar, J. D., Hamilton, R. A., Kuiken, T., Lentzos, F., Mampuys, R., Merad, M., Novossiolova, T., Oye, K., Perkins, E., Garcia-Reyero, N., Rhodes, C., & Linkov, I. (2020). Building biosecurity for synthetic biology. Molecular systems biology, 16(7), e9723. https://doi.org/10.15252/msb.20209723

3) James P. Stack, Richard M. Bostock, Raymond Hammerschmidt, Jeffrey B. Jones, and Eileen Luke. 2014. The National Plant Diagnostic Network: Partnering to Protect Plant Systems. Plant Disease / Vol. 98 No. 6. Published Online:12 May 2014. https://doi.org/10.1094/PDIS-08-13-0876-FE

4) CABI. (2023). PlantwisePlus: Knowledge for Better Plant Health. Wallingford, UK: CAB International.

5) (2023), Annual Report and Council Recommendations 2022. EPPO Bull, 53: 675-690. https://doi.org/10.1111/epp.12975

6) WTO. (2020). Sanitary and Phytosanitary Agreement: Legal Text. Geneva: World Trade Organization.

Chapter 7: Institutional Responses and Scientific Preparedness in India

1) National Disaster Management Authority (NDMA). (2008). Guidelines on Management of Biological Disasters. Government of India.

2) Indian Council of Agricultural Research (ICAR). (2021). *Annual Report 2020-21.*

3) Food Safety and Standards Authority of India (FSSAI). (2023). Food Safety Compliance System (FoSCoS) Annual Review.

4) Defence Research and Development Organisation (DRDO). (2021). DRDO Annual Report 2020-21. Ministry of Defence, Government of India.

5) Plant Quarantine (Regulation of Import into India) Order. (2003). Ministry of Agriculture & Farmers Welfare, Government of India.

6) The Prevention and Control of Infectious and Contagious Diseases in Animals Act, 2009, MINISTRY OF FISHERIES, ANIMAL HUSBANDRY & DAIRYING, GOVERNMENT OF INDIA.

7) Ministry of Agriculture & Farmers Welfare. (2023). Contingency Plans for Managing Extreme Events

Chapter 8: Policy Recommendations and Strategic Roadmap

1) Adhikari, P., Kumar, R., Iyengar, S. R. S., & Kaur, R. (2021). What a million Indian farmers say? A crowdsourcing-based method for pest surveillance. arXiv. https://doi.org/10.48550/arXiv.2108.03374

2) Australian Department of Agriculture & Water Resources. (2018). Farm Biosecurity Manual for the Organic Grains Industry. Canberra: Australian Government.

3) National Disaster Management Authority. (2008). Guidelines on Management of Biological Disasters. Government of India.

4) Press Information Bureau. (2024, August 16). Agriculture ministry launches national app to collect info on pest attacks in crops. Government of India. https://www.pib.gov.in/PressReleasePage.aspx?PRID=2114896

5) Times of India. (2024, November 11). DRDO boosts India's biosecurity with new BSL-4 laboratory. Times of India. https://timesofindia.indiatimes.com/city/bhopal/drdo-boosts-indias-biosecurity-with-new-bsl-4-laboratory-and-detection-facility/articleshow/115191760.cms

6) Gupta, K., & Sankaran, K. V. (2021). Forest biosecurity systems and processes: An Indian perspective. Frontiers in Forests and Global Change, 4, Article 699950. https://doi.org/10.3389/ffgc.2021.699950

Chapter 9: Legal Framework and Agroterrorism Law in India

1) Monke, J. (2005). Agroterrorism: Threats and Preparedness. Congressional Research Service Report for Congress.

2) NCRB. (2023). Accidental Deaths & Suicides in India – 2023. National Crime Records Bureau, Ministry of Home Affairs, Govt. of India.

3) Suby, S. B., Soujanya, P. L., Yadava, P., Patil, J., Subaharan, K., Prasad, G. S., Babu, K. S., Jat, S. L., Yathish, K. R., Vadassery, J., Kalia, V. K., Bakthavatsalam, N., Shekhar, J. C., & Rakshit, S. (2020). Invasion of fall armyworm (Spodoptera frugiperda) in India: nature, distribution, management and potential impact. Current Science, 119(1), 44–51. https://www.jstor.org/stable/27138850

4) UAPA. (1967). The Unlawful Activities (Prevention) Act, 1967. Ministry of Law and Justice, Government of India.

5) FAO. (2003). *Plant Quarantine (Regulation of Import into India) Order, 2003.* FAO/FAOLEX.

6) The White House. (2004). Homeland Security Presidential Directive/HSPD-9.

7) U.S. Congress. (2002). Public Health Security and Bioterrorism Preparedness and Response Act of 2002.

8) H.R.2122 - Project BioShield Act of 2003, 108th Congress (2003-2004)

About the Authors

1) Dr. Adesh Kumar

Associate Professor and Head, Department of Plant Pathology

Lovely Professional University, Punjab, India

President, Society for Precision Agriculture and Rural Innovation (SPARI)

Dr. Adesh Kumar currently serves as Associate Professor and Head of the Department of Plant Pathology at Lovely Professional University, Phagwara, Punjab, India. He is also the President of the Society for Precision Agriculture and Rural Innovation (SPARI), a national platform focused on integrating scientific innovation into rural development and sustainable agriculture. He earned his Ph.D. in Plant Pathology from Sardar Vallabhbhai Patel University of Agriculture and Technology, Meerut, in 2012. His primary research interests span Fungal Pathology, Biological Control of Phytopathogens, Plant-Microbe Interactions, and Microbial Decomposition. Over the course of his academic career, Dr. Kumar has authored more than 50 research and review articles, contributed over 10 book chapters, published 5 scholarly books, and holds 20+ patents and copyrights to his name.

Dr. Kumar has successfully mentored 40 undergraduates, 15 master's, and 1 Ph.D. student as both principal and co-supervisor. He has been recognized with several prestigious accolades, including the Young Scientist Award (2018), the Excellence in Research Award (2018), and most recently, the Excellence in Innovation Award (2025). He is an active member of esteemed scientific organizations, including the Indian Science Congress Association (ISCA), Indian Phytopathological Society (IPS), Madhumita Foundation, and Agricultural Technology Development Society (ATDS). Dr. Kumar has played key roles as Convener, Coordinator, Secretary, Session Chair, Judge, and Committee Head in various national and international conferences, symposia, and scientific congresses. Through his leadership and research contributions, Dr. Adesh Kumar continues to drive innovation in the field of plant pathology and agricultural resilience, with a particular emphasis on combating emerging biotic threats through sustainable and precision-based approaches.

2) Mr. Dibyendu Nayak

B.Sc. (Hons.) Agriculture, 2nd Year Student

Lovely Professional University, Phagwara, Punjab, India

Chief Executive Officer, Society for Precision Agriculture and Rural Innovation (SPARI)

Mr. Dibyendu Nayak is a second-year undergraduate student pursuing B.Sc. (Hons.) in Agriculture at Lovely Professional University, Phagwara, Punjab, India. He currently serves as the Chief Executive Officer of the Society for Precision Agriculture and Rural Innovation (SPARI), an organization committed to advancing innovative solutions in sustainable farming, agri-technology, and rural transformation. Formerly the Head of the Research Cell at Agri Nexus, a prominent student-led agricultural organization, Dibyendu has demonstrated strong leadership in fostering youth-led innovation. He is the Founder and former CEO of AgriNova India, which has now evolved into SPARI. Under his leadership, AgriNova India conceptualized and developed the HelioHive Lumitherm Project—a pathbreaking innovation that integrates solar-powered intelligent shielding systems for beekeeping, blending Artificial Intelligence with precision apiculture. The p0o9iuHelioHive Lumitherm Project has been recognized at various prestigious platforms:

- 1st Prize, Spring Flower Show 2025 (May)
- 1st Runner-Up, Inter-Hostel Science Project Competition 2025 (April)
- 1st Runner-Up, INNOTEK-2025, Agriculture & Allied Sciences Category (April)

He is also a consistent participant in academic and technical events such as Agrithon, Florithon, and INNOTEK 2025, showcasing his commitment to interdisciplinary innovation.

Beyond science and agriculture, Dibyendu is a talented artist and cultural enthusiast. He was honored with the Rashtriya Pratibha Samman 2025 for Nature and Lifestyle Photography by the Worthy Wellness Foundation. He also holds a Junior Diploma in Indian Classical Music and Rabindra sangeet from Prayag Sangeet Samiti, reflecting a rare blend of scientific curiosity and cultural depth.

As a young thought leader and systems innovator, Dibyendu Nayak continues to build bridges between rural resilience, technological advancement, and youth-driven change in Indian agriculture.

3) Ms. Vartika Singh

Ph.D. Scholar, Department of Botany

Lovely Professional University, Phagwara, Punjab, India

Chief of Research and Innovation Wing, Society for Precision Agriculture and Rural Innovation (SPARI)

Ms. Vartika Singh is currently pursuing her Ph.D. in Botany at Lovely Professional University, Phagwara, Punjab, India. She is the Chief of the Research and Innovation Wing of the Society for Precision Agriculture and Rural Innovation (SPARI), where she actively contributes to research planning, scientific strategy, and interdisciplinary knowledge creation within the agricultural sciences. With a strong academic foundation, Vartika has completed her postgraduate degree in Botany and has also successfully qualified some of India's most prestigious national-level examinations, including the CSIR-NET JRF and GATE, both of which underscore her commitment to scientific rigor and excellence. Her scholarly focus lies at the intersection of plant sciences, ecological resilience, and biosecurity, and she brings a structured yet accessible approach to complex scientific ideas. Her role in authoring this book reflects a deep desire to make critical knowledge about agroterrorism, biosecurity, and sustainable agriculture available to a wider audience, especially students and early-career researchers.

Vartika is passionate about making science both informative and inspiring, and she believes in empowering the next generation of researchers through well-curated, interdisciplinary learning. Her writing style blends academic clarity with conceptual depth, aimed at fostering curiosity, critical thinking, and practical application in the field of agro-environmental studies.

4) Dr. Hina Upadhyay

Associate Professor, Department of Agronomy

Lovely Professional University, Punjab, India

Vice-President, Society for Precision Agriculture and Rural Innovation (SPARI)

Dr. Hina Upadhyay is an Associate Professor in the Department of Agronomy at Lovely Professional University, Punjab, India, and currently serves as the Vice-President of the Society for Precision Agriculture and Rural Innovation (SPARI). With a distinguished academic and research career, she has previously worked as an Assistant Professor in the Department of Life Sciences at Boston College and Jiwaji University, Gwalior. From 1996 to 1998, she was a project fellow in the Aerobiology Laboratory at the School of Studies in Plant Sciences, Jiwaji University. A committed member of several scientific bodies, she is affiliated with the Association of Microbiologists of India, the Society of Bionaturalists (Fellow), the Indian Botanical Society, and the Indian Science Congress Association, where she served as a sectional member for Agriculture (2019–2020). She has chaired sessions and presented research at various national and international conferences and was a Board of Studies member in Botany at Jiwaji University from 2010 to 2013. Dr. Upadhyay has published over 45 peer-reviewed research and review articles, contributed 10 book chapters with Springer and Elsevier, and submitted 6 patent ideas along with funded projects to government agencies. Her contributions to science and education have earned her the XIII M.P. Young Scientist Award (1998), Best Teacher Award by Bharat Vikas Parishad (2005), and Women Researcher Award by INSO (2021). She established a vermicompost and agricultural waste management unit under the experiential learning program at LPU and actively mentors students in sustainable agroecosystem practices. Her research focuses on integrated nutrient management, biopesticides, biopriming, and eco-friendly solutions for sustainable crop production.

5) Mr. Sounak Chakraborty

B.Sc. (Hons.) Agriculture, 2nd Year Student

Lovely Professional University, Phagwara, Punjab, India

Expert, Research and Innovation Wing, Society for Precision Agriculture and Rural Innovation (SPARI)

Mr. Sounak Chakraborty is currently pursuing his B.Sc. (Hons.) in Agriculture at Lovely Professional University, Phagwara, Punjab. He serves as an Expert in the Research and Innovation Wing of the Society for Precision Agriculture and Rural Innovation (SPARI), contributing to the organization's focus on agricultural resilience, sustainability, and strategic innovation. Hailing from West Bengal, Sounak completed his schooling from Santipur Municipal High School, where he laid the academic foundation for his ongoing journey in agricultural sciences. His current academic interests lie in the field of risk management, particularly focusing on international frameworks for agricultural biosecurity and policy resilience.

Sounak has also developed a strong interest in mushroom farming, exploring both its practical and commercial aspects, and aspires to integrate modern techniques with traditional practices to support sustainable agri-entrepreneurship. As a member of the SPARI team, he actively contributes to literature development and policy research, bringing a fresh perspective to agro-environmental issues with a strong commitment to grassroots impact and rural innovation.

6) Mr. Furquan Khalid

B.Sc. (Hons.) Agriculture, 2nd Year Student

Lovely Professional University, Phagwara, Punjab, India

Chief Marketing Officer, Department of Marketing, Society for Precision Agriculture and Rural Innovation (SPARI)

Mr. Furquan Khalid is currently pursuing his B.Sc. (Hons.) in Agriculture at Lovely Professional University, Phagwara, Punjab, and serves as the Chief Marketing Officer of the Society for Precision Agriculture and Rural Innovation (SPARI). In this role, he leads marketing and outreach efforts for cutting-edge agricultural innovations and grassroots engagement initiatives. He brings strong leadership, strategic planning, and communication skills to his work, complemented by a solid foundation in Microsoft Office tools and data visualization platforms. He is passionate about combining technology with practical farming knowledge to drive transformation in rural sectors. He has participated in multiple innovation events, including the Smart India Hackathon (SIH) and a 36-hour hackathon at LPU, where he showcased his drive for solving real-world problems through interdisciplinary collaboration. One of his most notable achievements includes conceptualizing and developing Vita Guard, an AI-enabled, implantable health monitoring system capable of detecting vital changes and notifying healthcare providers in real time. The system employs bioimpedance sensors, flow cytometry, and advanced IoT-machine learning frameworks, showcasing his interest in health-tech and agritech convergence. He has been awarded District First in Kabaddi, recognized for his excellence in healthcare and welfare innovation under Central Government Act-21,1860, and certified in Advanced Microsoft Excel from MindLuster.

Furquan represents a new generation of agricultural professionals who combine technical innovation, field knowledge, and strategic outreach to help shape a resilient and smart agricultural future.

7) Mr. Anindya Sanyal

B.Sc. (Hons.) Agriculture, 2nd Year Student

Lovely Professional University, Phagwara, Punjab, India

Expert, Research and Innovation Wing, Society for Precision Agriculture and Rural Innovation (SPARI)

Mr. Anindya Sanyal is a second-year B.Sc. (Hons.) Agriculture student at Lovely Professional University, Phagwara, Punjab. He currently serves as an Expert in the Research and Innovation Wing of the Society for Precision Agriculture and Rural Innovation (SPARI), where he contributes to experimental design and field-based agri-technology assessments. Originally from West Bengal, Anindya completed his 10th from Usagram Boys' High School and 12th from Indian Convent School. His academic interests lie in insect pest biology, plant health, and sustainable irrigation systems. He holds specialized knowledge in the breeding and lifecycle control of the rice mill moth (Corcyra cephalonica) and has growing expertise in drip irrigation systems tailored to optimize water efficiency in resource-scarce agricultural regions.

A passionate learner, Anindya is also deeply enthusiastic about plant pathology and strives to bridge scientific knowledge with practical farming applications. He is proficient in Microsoft Excel, PowerPoint, Word, and marketing communications—skills he uses to support the outreach and technical documentation initiatives within SPARI.

Driven by curiosity and dedication, Mr. Anindya Sanyal aims to contribute to a new era of sustainable, intelligent, and pest-resilient agriculture.